THE
MODERN
WORLD

Brian Williams
Illustrated by James Field

PETER BEDRICK BOOKS
NEW YORK

TIMELINK: THE MODERN WORLD

PETER BEDRICK BOOKS
2112 Broadway
New York, New York 10023

Copyright © Reed International Books Ltd 1993

Designed and produced by Lionheart Books

Artwork by James Field

Published by agreement with Reed International
Books Ltd

Library of Congress Cataloging-in-Publication
Data

Williams, Brian, 1943-
    Modern World / Brian Williams; illustrated by
    James Field.
    64p. 28 × 21.4 cm -- (Timelink)
    Includes index.
    ISBN 0-87226-312-6
    1. History, Modern -- Juvenile literature. [1.
    History, Modern.] I. Field, James, 1959- ill.
    II. Title.   III. Series.
    D208W53   1994
    909.08--dc20   94-18458
                                        CIP

Printed in China
97 96 95 94 1 2 3 4

A new post-World War II
standard of living in the
USA in the 1950s – see
pages 44 and 45.

CONTENTS

Left: Guglielmo Marconi
pioneers the
development of radio –
see page 29.

INTRODUCTION

This book is an introduction to the greatest events in world history during the modern era. This begins with the French Revolution and Napoleon Bonaparte, the expansion of the United States, and the spread of the Industrial Revolution. The book is divided into seven chapters arranged in time sequence from 1789 to the 1990s. Each chapter includes an overview of world events, short features on important wars, revolutions and social changes, with extended features on subjects such as the American Civil War, the colonial era in Africa in the 1800s, the rise of the dictators in the 1920s and 1930s, the Space Age, and the dramatic world events of recent decades.

Modern World is the fourth title in the Timelink series, which is designed to give young readers an overall view of different peoples and their histories, and the links between states and civilizations across the world. One book cannot describe in detail all that happened everywhere in the world during a period of tremendous change, but this book does show many of the significant turning points that shaped the world we live in today.

Throughout the **Modern World** there are maps, illustrations, diagrams, photographs and timecharts. The maps show the rise and fall of empires, the emergence of new nations from wars and revolutions, the changes in

Below: Railways, bridges and factories – scene from a 19th-century European city.

the balance of power. The illustrations help bring to life dramatic events and show how people lived – their clothes, buildings, arts and sciences, and everyday activities. The timecharts list the dates of important events around the world. At the back of the book are two larger timecharts covering the whole of the period, and a Glossary of words that may be unfamiliar to young readers.

Finding out about the past

From the 1800s we have new and exciting sources of information about the changing world. No longer do we need to rely on just books, drawings and paintings to bring alive the past. First came photographs. Later,

sound recordings and films, followed by radio and television, became available to save and store the sights and sounds of history being made.

Many of the famous people whose achievements shaped the Modern World wrote about their own lives and times. Such books are called autobiographies. With diaries, newspapers and government papers, they are valuable sources for historians. So too are biographies, books written by other people about the famous. From all this evidence, in words and pictures, you can judge for yourself the effect of the events – often dramatic and terrible – which shaped the Modern World.

DATES AND PERIODS

All the dates in this book are based on a calendar which has the birth of Jesus Christ as its starting point. Events happening after the birth of Christ are counted forwards from it. They are given the letters AD from the Latin words *anno domini*, meaning 'in the year of the Lord'. In **Modern World** all the dates are AD.

Wars and revolutions

In this book, you will come across references to numerous wars. Some were local wars, between rival nations. Some were civil wars, between opposing groups within a nation. Two are known as

World Wars: the First World War (1914–18) and the Second World War (1939–45). These wars, also known as World War I and World War II, were the most destructive wars in history. Fighting, with new and increasingly deadly weapons, involved many countries and spread around the world.

You will also read about revolutions. A revolution is a 'turning around', which in history means a time of great changes, affecting the way countries are governed and the way people live. Important revolutions in **Modern World** include the French Revolution, the Industrial Revolution, the Russian Revolution, and the Technology Revolution.

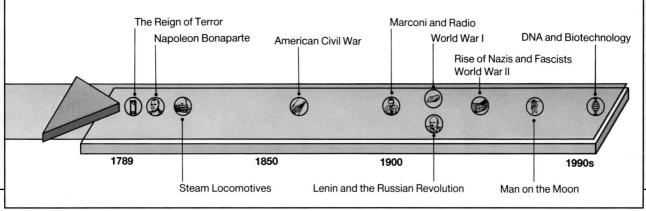

The Reign of Terror
Napoleon Bonaparte
American Civil War
Marconi and Radio
World War I
DNA and Biotechnology
Rise of Nazis and Fascists
World War II

1789   1850   1900   1990s

Steam Locomotives   Lenin and the Russian Revolution   Man on the Moon

THE CHANGING WORLD

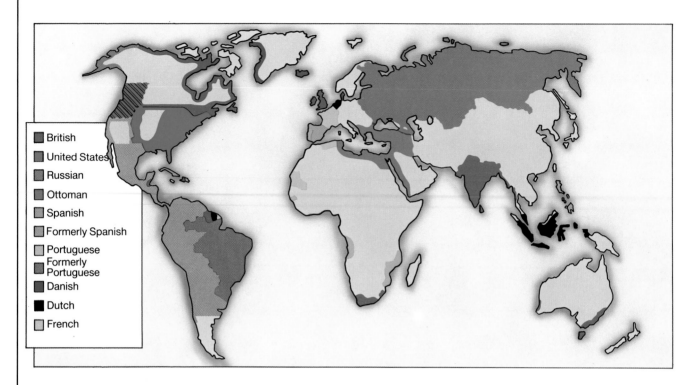

British
United States
Russian
Ottoman
Spanish
Formerly Spanish
Portuguese
Formerly Portuguese
Danish
Dutch
French

▲ THE WORLD REFORMED 1789–1830

Napoleon fashioned a new Europe. After his defeat, politicians tried unsuccessfully to restore the old. Revolutionary ideas inspired revolts in Europe and South America. The Industrial Revolution brought even greater changes in people's lives.

▼ GREAT POWER RIVALRY 1880s

The Great Powers were rivals for colonies, trade and influence. Britain's navy guarded its overseas empire; Russia tried to control a huge land empire. Germany and Japan were rising powers. Migrants from Europe sought new lives in the ever-developing United States.

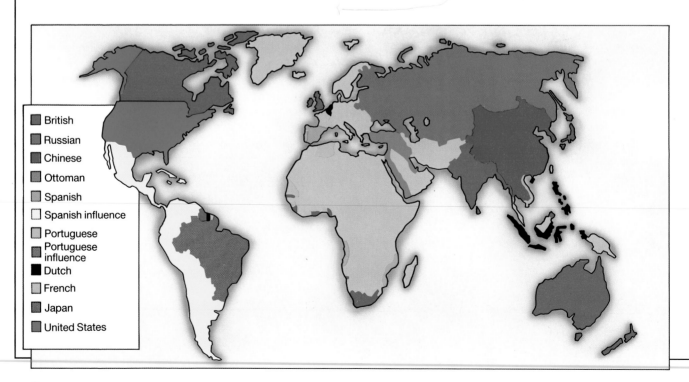

British
Russian
Chinese
Ottoman
Spanish
Spanish influence
Portuguese
Portuguese influence
Dutch
French
Japan
United States

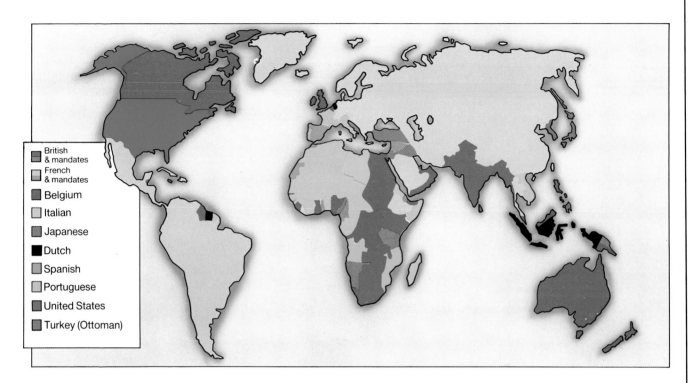

British
& mandates
French
& mandates
Belgium
Italian
Japanese
Dutch
Spanish
Portuguese
United States
Turkey (Ottoman)

▲ THE WORLD AFTER WAR 1920

The Great War (1914–18) was the first world war. It left France and Germany weak, and Britain exhausted. Russia had the world's first Communist government. China was a republic. After the war, the United States was strong, but tried to stay out of world affairs.

▼ THE WORLD IN THE 1990s

The USA is the only military superpower. Asia becomes more powerful, especially in trade. The USSR has broken up, but Europe moves towards economic unity. As population grows rapidly, people face the problems of environmental damage, poverty and famine.

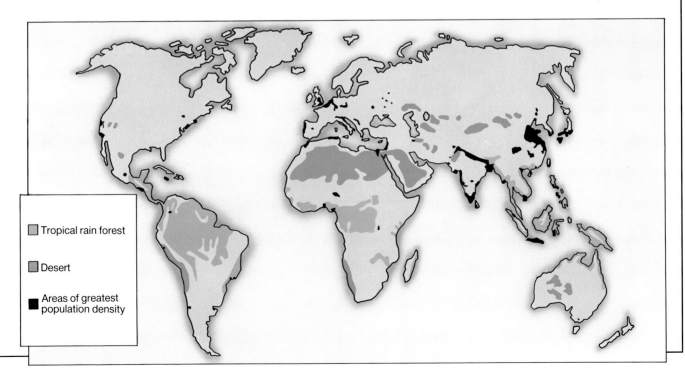

Tropical rain forest

Desert

Areas of greatest
population density

REVOLUTION AND WAR

In 1789 the tidal wave of revolution broke on French shores. Earlier, across the Atlantic, revolution had forged a new nation: the United States. Now, in France, the collapse of the old order sent shock waves through a continent. They were to spread far and wide, to South America and beyond.

For two years the fate of the French monarchy hung in the balance. Then, in 1791, the royal family tried to escape from France. The king was captured, and imprisoned on charges of treason. A new assembly, the National Convention, declared France a republic.

In 1793 King Louis XVI and his Queen Marie-Antoinette were executed on the guillotine. A bloody reign of terror began (see right). As enthusiastic revolutionaries offered aid to uprisings in other countries, France became engaged in wars lasting until 1815. A French general, Napoleon Bonaparte, seized power in 1799, when his country was threatened by an alliance of Britain, Russia, Austria and Prussia. By 1804 Bonaparte had crowned himself Emperor of France.

▽ Europe was at war. The USA expanded westward. South America freed itself from Spain and Portugal. European settlement of Australia began. Japan and China remained aloof.

⊙ THE REIGN OF TERROR

In 1790 Dr Guillotin, a supporter of the French Revolution, suggested an improved method of execution. His invention, the guillotine, was well used during France's Reign of Terror. In 1792 the National Convention abolished the monarchy; within months Louis XVI had been executed. Many other heads rolled too. Uncompromising revolutionaries, called Jacobins, seized power. A Committee of Public Safety ruled France; its aim was to root out 'enemies of the people' and execute them. The leading Jacobin was Maximilien Robespierre. As many as 25,000 people died in the Terror, including Robespierre himself in 1794.

Revolutionaries use the guillotine

Exploring the US

Guillotine

Napoleon

Volta's battery

War in the US

Steam locomotives

Romantic Movement

Science & Medicine

⊙ EXPLORING THE WEST

In 1804 Meriwether Lewis and William Clark set out to explore the north-western wilderness of the United States. They wanted to find a coast-to-coast trade route and to record the region's people, wildlife and minerals. Their 45-strong party canoed from St Louis up the Missouri River, through Louisiana and the little-known Oregon region. They crossed the Rocky Mountains with help from Sacagawea, a woman of the Shoshone tribe. The expedition reached the Pacific and returned in September 1806. It enabled the United States to claim Oregon, opening the way to the West for the pioneers of the 1800s.

Lewis and Clark map the West

⊙ WAR OF 1812

As part of its campaign against Napoleon, the British navy stopped foreign ships around its territories. Interference with shipping hurt US trade. In 1812 the United States went to war with Britain over this, though Britain had in fact already changed its policy. The Americans won a naval victory on Lake Erie in 1813 and tried to invade Canada. In 1814 the British captured the US capital, Washington, and burned the White House, Capitol and navy yard. The war ended in 1815 with a British defeat at New Orleans – two weeks after the two countries had signed a peace treaty in Europe, news of which arrived too late to prevent the battle.

The battle of Lake Erie

America grows

In 1789, the year of the outbreak of the French Revolution, George Washington became the first President of the United States of America. The Americans could not make up their minds as to which side to support in the European war, France or Britain, or whether to fight at all. Washington decided that America should stay at peace, since it had a new federal government to get used to and new lands to survey.

In 1803 the United States added more than 780,000 square miles of land to its area, by buying the Louisiana territory from France. President Thomas Jefferson sent Meriwether Lewis and William Clark to explore the newly acquired land and what lay beyond (see above).

1789–1800
1789 Start of French Revolution.
1789 George Washington first US President.
1791 Canada Act: Britain divides Canada.
1791 Toussaint l'Ouverture leads slave revolt in Haiti against the French.
1792 Gustavus III of Sweden assassinated.
1792 Gas lighting invented.
1793 Execution of French king Louis XVI.
1795 British take Cape of Good Hope from Dutch.
1796 Death of Catherine the Great of Russia.
1798 French invade Egypt.
1799 Bonaparte sets up consulate in France.
1799 Washington dies.
1800 Robert Fulton builds a submarine (USA).

1800–1815
1800 First electric battery, by Alessandro Volta.
1800 Russia takes control of Georgia.
1801 Russian tsar Paul I murdered.
1802 Peace of Amiens halts war in Europe.
1803 USA gains Louisiana.
1804 Bonaparte crowned Emperor Napoleon I.
1804 First steam locomotive.
1805 Battle of Trafalgar.
1807 Slavery abolished in the British Empire.
1808–14 Peninsular War.
1810 Argentina independent from Spain.
1812 War between Britain and the USA.
1812 Napoleon invades Russia.
1814 Napoleon in exile.
1815 Battle of Waterloo. Congress of Vienna.

▼ NAPOLEON, SOLDIER–EMPEROR

Napoleon Bonaparte was born in 1769 on the Mediterranean island of Corsica, which had been French territory for just a year. Bonaparte made his name as a soldier in Italy, and in France, where his cannon in the streets of Paris saved the revolutionary government. In 1798 he invaded Egypt, but his army was stranded after a French naval defeat by the British. France's government was weak. Napoleon returned to a hero's welcome and seized power. As a general, Napoleon seemed unbeatable: in the course of his campaigns he outfought the Austrians, Prussians and Russians. By 1804 he was crowned Emperor of France, and the world lay at his feet. But he made two fateful mistakes. He let his generals become involved in a long, losing campaign in Spain and Portugal (1808–14), and he invaded Russia (1812), with the loss of most of his Grand Army.

Napoleon's Russian campaign

NAPOLEON

1769 Born at Ajaccio, Corsica.
1793 Defends Toulon.
1795 Disperses rebels in Paris. Commands army in France.
1796 Marries Josephine de Beauharnais. Commands army in Italy.
1798 Invades Egypt.
1799 Returns to France, makes himself First Consul.
1802 Begins reforms in France.
1804 Crowned Emperor.
1809 Divorces Josephine, marries Marie-Louise of Austria.
1812 Russian campaign.
1814 Forced to abdicate, exiled to Elba.
1815 Returns to France, but defeated at Waterloo.
1821 Dies on St Helena.

▷ Napoleon (right) was known by his soldiers as the Little Corporal (he did not shirk from aiming cannon himself). Napoleon won battles by skilful use of artillery and mass attack by foot-soldiers and cavalry against the enemy's weakest spot. His hopes of invading Britain were dashed in 1805 when Britain's Admiral Nelson defeated the French and Spanish fleets at Trafalgar.

EUROPE

1789 French Revolution.
1792 France at war.
1793 French king executed.
1793 Second partition of Poland, by Russia and Prussia.
1794 The Terror in France.
1795 Third partition of Poland, between Russia, Prussia and Austria.
1799 Napoleon seizes power in France.
1800 Ireland enters political union with Great Britain.
1801 Alexander I, tsar of Russia.
1802 Treaty of Amiens; Britain and France at peace.
1804 Napoleon becomes Emperor of France.
1806 End of Holy Roman Empire.
1808–14 Peninsular War.
1812 Napoleon invades Russia.
1813 French defeated at battle of Leipzig.
1814 Allies invade France, Napoleon abdicates.
1815 Napoleon defeated. Congress of Vienna.

The battle of Trafalgar

The United States could not escape the effects of war in Europe. In 1812 a quarrel with Britain over trade led to a short war (see page 9).

Trade and industry

The period of the Napoleonic Wars (see pages 10 and 14–15) saw many social and industrial changes. Napoleon was a modernizer who was keenly interested in new developments, such as the electric battery (see right). The industrial revolution was accelerating, especially in Britain, which was fast becoming a land of factories. New power looms in the textile mills were steam-driven, speeding up production and putting the hand-loom weavers out of work. By 1800 some 500 steam engines of James Watt's design were working in Britain. Trade boomed while war raged in Europe. British mills even produced the cloth that was made up into uniforms for French soldiers.

Revolt and suppression

Many people in Britain and elsewhere in Europe supported the ideals of the French Revolution. They campaigned for the abolition of slavery. They cheered news of a black revolt in Haiti. They welcomed Argentina's break with Spain. Opponents of the Revolution pointed to the cruelty and mass killings.

⊛ VOLTA AND THE BATTERY

Volta's 'pile'

Count Alessandro Volta, an Italian scientist, demonstrated his electrical 'pile' to France's ruler Napoleon in 1801. This was the first battery. In a salt solution, Volta stacked pairs of metal plates (one zinc, one silver), separated by cardboard discs. The chemical reaction caused produced electricity.

ASIA	AFRICA	AMERICA	PACIFIC
1792 China invades Nepal. **1793** Britain sends Lord Macartney on an unsuccessful diplomatic mission to China. **1793** Law courts in India reorganized on British model by Governor-General Cornwallis. **1794** Aga Muhammad founds Qaja dynasty in Persia. **1796** Britain captures Ceylon (Sri Lanka) from the Dutch. **1797** Japan reopens trade links with outside world. **1799** British take control of South India, after death of Tipu Sahib, ruler of Mysore. **1800** Persian empire loses border territory to Russia. **1803** British fight Marathas in India. **1804** Japanese refuse to allow Russians to open a trade base in Japan. **1808** China bans Christian books and pamphlets. **1811** British occupy Java.	**1795** Britain takes Cape of Good Hope from the Dutch. **1795** Mungo Park (Scottish) explores the Gambia and Niger rivers in West Africa. **1798** War in South Africa between Boers and Xhosas. **1799** Rosetta Stone discovered by French in Egypt; its inscriptions decode the mystery of Egyptian hieroglyphics. **1804** Fulanis conquer Hausa rivals in West Africa. **1805** Muhammad Ali is made pasha (governor) of Egypt by the Ottoman sultan. **1807** Slavery abolished within British Empire. Sierra Leone and Gambia become British colonies. **1810** Chaka, Zulu leader, begins organizing *impis* (trained armies). **1811** Mameluke rulers of Egypt massacred on orders of Muhammad Ali. **1815** Boer farmers rebel in Cape colony.	**1789** George Washington is the first US President. **1791** Britain divides Canada into French- and English-speaking territories. Slave revolt in Haiti. **1791** US Bill of Rights, the first 10 amendments to the Constitution. **1801–4** Alexander von Humboldt of Germany explores South America. **1801–9** Thomas Jefferson is US President. **1803** Purchase of Louisiana almost doubles the size of the USA. **1804** Lewis and Clark expedition **1808** Shawnee chief Tecumseh attempts to forge an Indian league. **1810** Argentina independent. **1811** Venezuela and Paraguay declare independence, followed, in 1812, by Colombia. **1812** Britain and the USA at war. **1814** Mexican revolution. **1815** Americans defeat British at New Orleans.	**1791** Sealers and whalers visit coast of New Zealand. First European missionaries land. Flax and timber trade begins. Third British fleet arrives in Australia. **1792** New South Wales Corps, Australia's first immigrant government, set up. **1801–3** Matthew Flinders' voyage on the *Investigator* is the first circumnavigation of the Australian continent. **1803** Van Diemen's Land (Tasmania) founded as a penal colony for transported criminals. **1808** The Rum Rebellion. William Bligh, British governor of New South Wales, is deposed and replaced by Lachlan Macquarie. **1813** Blue Mountains north of Sydney, Australia crossed for the first time by British settlers. **1814** Samuel Marsden sets up an Anglican mission station at Bay Islands, New Zealand.

Governments feared that any unrest at home might lead to revolution on their soil, and so took harsh action against protest movements. Some British workers, afraid of losing their jobs to machines, smashed factory equipment. They were called Luddites, after their imaginary leader 'Ned Ludd'.

Events In Asia

In the East, any news of the turmoil in the West that reached so far was of little interest or made no impact. The people of Japan had their own problems with food shortages. Meanwhile India was coming increasingly under British rule. There were new British-style law courts, and by 1800 Britain had extended its control to southern India.

China, the largest nation on Earth, with over 300 million people, spurned envoys from the West. The proud Manchu emperor, who believed that China was the world's only true civilization, was more concerned with putting down uprisings by local bandits and suppressing subject countries such as Nepal and Vietnam.

The Muslim world, Australia, Africa

The once-great Muslim empires were now in decline. Persia and Ottoman Turkey were weakening, while Mogul India had all but passed into history. Turkey still held lands, including Greece, in eastern Europe, but faced mounting nationalist unrest that was inspired by the example of France.

In Australia, the first white settlers (mainly convicts from Britain) were building farms and towns. Matthew Flinders made the first voyage around the coastline of Australia (1803), while earlier, in West Africa, the Scottish explorer Mungo Park traced the course of the Niger River (1795). In South Africa, Britain took over Cape Colony from the Dutch. Another new power was also rising in southern Africa – the Zulus.

A new age dawns

In 1804 an important technological advance was made by Richard Trevithick, a British engineer. He built the first steam rail locomotive (see page 13). Also in the early 1800s, the American steamship pioneer Robert Fulton designed a submarine, which he offered to France, as a weapon. The French refused it, but accepted a process invented by their countryman, Nicolas Appert, for keeping food fresh, by boiling it in glass jars. Napoleon's army first adopted this idea.

John Dalton of Britain and Amedeo Avogadro of Italy made important advances in understanding atoms and how they combine to form molecules. In medicine, surgery improved, and Edward Jenner pioneered inoculation against smallpox. By the end of the Napoleonic wars, there was gas lighting on some European city streets, and the age of electricity was about to begin (see page 11).

▼ ROMANTIC MOVEMENT

The Romantic movement in the arts and philosophy began in Europe in the late 1700s. Poets and painters turned away from the 'rules' of Classical (Greek–Roman) style. They believed in freedom, imagination and the power of Nature. Some Romantics were revolutionaries. Others found inspiration in medieval tales and folklore. Leading Romantic writers included Goethe in Germany and Wordsworth in Britain. There were Romantic painters (Delacroix, Constable) and Romantic composers (Beethoven, Chopin). Most Romantics distrusted the new age of machines.

Romantic painting by Caspar-David Friedrich 1819

▶ STEAM LOCOMOTIVE

Engineers had worked with steam pumping engines in the 1700s. A steam-powered vehicle needed a smaller engine, using steam at higher pressure. Richard Trevithick learned about steam engines from their use in the Cornish tin mines. In 1801 he built a high-pressure steam carriage, and drove it along the road. In 1803 he built the world's first steam railway locomotive, which could haul 10 tons of iron and 70 men. In 1808 Trevithick's 'Catch-me-who can' puffed around a track in London, before the amazed spectators.

Trevithick's locomotive

▼ SCIENCE AND MEDICINE

Science made many advances in the early 19th century. Physicians pioneered improved surgical techniques. Inoculation against disease was proved to work. But hygiene in hospitals was poor, and operations were dangerous. Amputations (without anaesthetics) could kill patients from shock or infection. There was a breakthrough in the understanding and use of electromagnetism. The young Michael Faraday, who later invented the dynamo and electric motor, worked in London assisting Humphry Davy, inventor of the miner's safety lamp (1815).

A ship's surgeon at work

Faraday in his laboratory

THE NAPOLEONIC WARS

France, in 1792, was a country in upheaval, fighting to defend the revolution at home and to spread the revolutionary message abroad. After a period of government by a succession of rival committees in France, Napoleon Bonaparte led his army in a coup to save the revolution. As a soldier, he offered a simple message, 'follow me'.

Napoleon the reformer
France needed peace, to rebuild and reform. At home, Napoleon governed well. He introduced a new code of laws and made France's government more efficient. He founded the Bank of France. The Catholic Church, which had been persecuted by the revolutionaries, was allowed to regain its place in national life. More schools were built, and wider education was encouraged.

The European campaigns
But Napoleon dreamed of greater glory. He wanted a French-dominated Europe, with his own relatives as its rulers. From 1803 until 1814 he led France to war.

At first, he scored a succession of victories: 1805 Austerlitz (over Russia and Austria), 1806 Jena (over Prussia), 1807 Friedland (over Russia), 1809 Wagram (over Austria). Only the British navy remained unbeaten. Napoleon tried to strangle Britain's trade by blockade, but he failed.

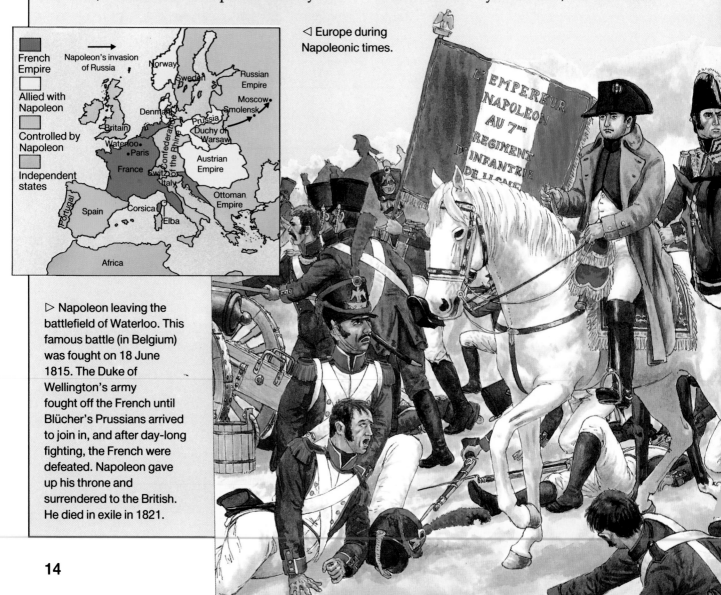

◁ Europe during Napoleonic times.

French Empire

Allied with Napoleon

Controlled by Napoleon

Independent states

Napoleon's invasion of Russia

Norway
Sweden
Russian Empire
Moscow
Smolensk
Denmark
Britain
Prussia
Duchy of Warsaw
Waterloo
Paris
Confederation of the Rhine
Austrian Empire
France
Switzerland
Italy
Ottoman Empire
Portugal
Spain
Corsica
Elba
Africa

▷ Napoleon leaving the battlefield of Waterloo. This famous battle (in Belgium) was fought on 18 June 1815. The Duke of Wellington's army fought off the French until Blücher's Prussians arrived to join in, and after day-long fighting, the French were defeated. Napoleon gave up his throne and surrendered to the British. He died in exile in 1821.

△ Napoleon in his study, painted by Jacques Louis David, a supporter of the French Revolution. David also painted Napoleon's coronation.

▷ At the Congress of Vienna, Europe's leading statesmen tried to restore the old order and put back the map of Europe as it had been before Napoleon's grand designs. The four Congress leaders were Metternich (Austria), Castlereagh (Britain), Tsar Alexander I (Russia) and Talleyrand (France).

NAPOLEON'S WARS

1796 Defeats Austrians in Italy.
1798 Egypt: wins Battle of the Pyramids against Mamelukes.
1800 Crosses Alps, defeats Austrians at Marengo.
1805 Defeats Austrians at Ulm, Austrians and Russians at Austerlitz.
1806 Defeats Prussians at Jena.
1807 Defeats Russians at Friedland.
1809 Defeats Austrians at Wagram.
1812 Disaster in Russia.
1813 Defeated at Battle of the Nations, Germany.
1815 Disaster at Waterloo.

In the long Peninsular War (1808–14) fought in Spain and Portugal, Napoleon's generals were at last defeated. Then, in Russia, fierce resistance and the bitter snows of winter killed 500,000 French soldiers during their disastrous retreat from the captured city of Moscow (1812). In 1813 the French army was beaten at Leipzig in Germany, and France was then invaded. Napoleon was exiled to the island of Elba.

Less than a year later, Napoleon had regained his crown. His final defeat came at Waterloo in June 1815. Napoleon was sent to the South Atlantic, to die in lonely exile on St Helena.

In France, the monarchy was restored. At the Congress of Vienna the allied victors, led by the Austrian Count Metternich, tried to restore the old Europe. But Europe had changed, and there was no going back.

STRUGGLES FOR FREEDOM

The French Revolution was over, but its ideals – liberty, equality, brotherhood – lived on. In the 1820s and 1830s revolution spread, in Europe and the Americas. New nations fought for freedom after years of foreign rule. As Spain's empire fell apart, the modern countries of South America were created by militant patriots such as Simon Bolivar (see page 17). Turkey, called the 'sick man of Europe', was unable to hold on to its Balkan territories, which were eyed by its envious neighbour Russia. This conflict resulted in the Crimean War (see page 20).

Social change and revolution

In the West, the new industrial society rapidly transformed people's lives. Cities grew larger and more crowded (see pages 24–25), but most city dwellers had little say in how they were governed. In most countries, only wealthy men (such as landowners) had the right to vote. Women could not vote at all. The railway age was changing society (see page 17), but governments lagged far behind in ideas for making society better for all.

In 1830 France had a second revolution, replacing its Bourbon king with one chosen by the people. In 1848 – the 'year of revolutions' – uprisings spread across Europe. France became a republic again, with Louis Napoleon, Bonaparte's nephew, as president. Within four years, he had become emperor, like his uncle before him.

Most of the 1848 revolutions failed, but their supporters did not abandon the struggle. By 1861 the Italian nationalist movement led by Mazzini, Cavour and Garibaldi had succeeded in uniting most of Italy (see page 22). Elsewhere, the German founders of Communism, Marx and Engels, urged industrial workers to revolt against the factory system and the whole economic order.

Migration, gold and hunger

People were on the move. Across the United States, wagon trains of pioneers began rolling westward (see page 17). The California gold rush in 1848 sent thousands of eager gold-seekers west, over the Rocky Mountains and by sea around Cape Horn.

▽ Europe was industrializing and convulsed by freedom movements. The USA reached from the Atlantic to the Pacific, but was almost split by a civil war. Russia was gaining an eastern empire. India rebelled against British rule. Weak China was helpless against Western imperialist attack, and Japan was opened to Western trade.

1815–1840

1815 Congress of Vienna.
1818 British defeat Marathas in India.
1819 Raffles founds British colony of Singapore.
1820s Liberation struggles in South America.
1821 Michael Faraday invents electric dynamo.
1825 First passenger-carrying steam railway.
1830 Revolution in France; Second Republic.
1835 Boers begin Great Trek (South Africa).
1836 Texas wins independence from Mexico.
1838 First electric telegraph.
1839 Opium war between Britain and China.
1840 First postage stamps, Britain.
1840 New Zealand becomes a British colony.

1840–1865

1842 Britain takes Hong Kong from China.
1845 US–Mexican War.
1848 Revolutions across Europe.
1848 Californian gold rush.
1850 Taiping rebellion in China.
1852 Fall of Second Republic in France. Napoleon III becomes Emperor.
1854 USA forces Japan to open up to Western trade.
1854–6 Crimean War.
1857 Indian Mutiny.
1859 Darwin publishes ideas on evolution in *The Origin of Species*.
1860–1 Cavour and Garibaldi unite Italy.
1861 Pasteur shows that germs cause disease.
1861–5 American Civil War.
1865 Assassination of President Lincoln.

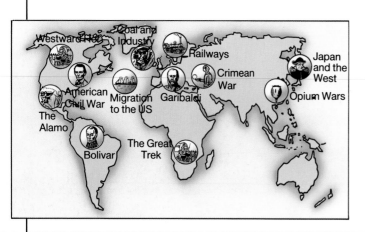

Westward Ho! · Coal and Industry · Railways · Japan and the West · Crimean War · Opium Wars · American Civil War · Migration to the US · Garibaldi · The Alamo · Bolivar · The Great Trek

Early railway passengers

Simon Bolivar

⏶ THE RAILWAY AGE

Railways were the technological marvels of the mid-1800s. Some people warned of the dangers to health of travelling faster than a galloping horse; others warned of passengers choking in smoke-filled tunnels. But the new steam trains puffed into the hearts of cities all over the world, and across mountains and plains. Cheap rail travel changed society, creating the city suburb and the day trip.

⏶ BOLIVAR AND FREEDOM

The Venezuelan Simon Bolivar (1783–1830) freed six South American nations from Spanish rule: Venezuela, Colombia, Ecuador, Peru, Panama and Bolivia (named after him). He led troops through the tropics, across the Andes and to victories over armies twice as large as his own. He helped set up the new nations and tried to form them into a union. When this aim failed, 'the Liberator' retired from public life.

⏷ WAGONS WESTWARD

Settlers heading west across the United States in the 1840s faced many hardships: hunger, thirst, disease, blistering heat, biting cold and attacks by Indians. Most settlers travelled in groups of as many as a hundred families. They formed a wagon train of 'prairie schooners', pulled by oxen or mules and crammed with their possessions. Along with the wagons went cattle and horses. Most wagon trains started in spring from Independence, Missouri, heading out across the Great Plains. The settlers hoped to reach California or Oregon in five months, before winter came.

A covered wagon rolls across the plain

Boers with Zulus

In South Africa, Boer farmers journeyed north in their wagons, seeking new land to settle. They fought the Zulus (see right).

Most poor people in Europe had little or no hope of escaping to a new world. Many lived in miserable slums. In mines and factories, women and children often did the dirtiest and most dangerous jobs (see page 19). A few laws were made to improve working conditions, but workers trying to start trade unions risked arrest.

Europe and North America were now the 'workshops' of the world. Slaves in the United States picked cotton, which was shipped to English mills, where workers made cloth for sale in Africa and India. In 1851, 6 million visitors crowded the halls of the Great Exhibition in London to marvel at the products of world trade and industry.

▲ THE GREAT TREK

In 1835 a party of Dutch-speaking farmers (Boers) moved north from Cape Colony, South Africa, across the Orange River to find new land. About 10,000 more *voortrekkers* (advance pioneers) followed over the next three years. These were families in ox-wagons making the long, hard Great Trek to the interior. They founded the Transvaal and Orange Free State. They claimed the lands across the Vaal River after conquering the local Ndebele people, while at the Battle of Blood River, 1838, they defeated the Zulus to settle in Natal.

EUROPE	ASIA	AFRICA	AMERICA
1820 Greek war of independence. **1822** End of Congress of Vienna. **1830** Belgium throws off Dutch rule. **1830** July Revolution in France. **1832** Reform Act in Britain: the middle classes get the vote. **1834** Civil war in Spain. **1836** Chartist reform movement. **1837** Queen Victoria comes to the throne in Britain. **1840** First penny post in Britain. **1846** Potato famine in Ireland. **1848** Revolutions throughout Europe. Most end in failure. Marx and Engels publish *The Communist Manifesto*. **1848** Second French Republic. **1851** Great Exhibition in London. **1852** Second French empire under Louis Napoleon (Napoleon III). **1854–6** Crimean War. **1861** Garibaldi and Cavour unite Italy. **1862** Bismarck becomes Chancellor of Prussia.	**1818** India: British defeat Marathas. **1819** Singapore founded. Ranjit Singh conquers Kashmir for the Sikhs. **1824** First British–Burmese War. **1825** Dutch defeat Javanese. **1830** Russia begins conquest of Kazakhstan. **1833** Muhammad Ali of Egypt gains Syria. **1838** War between Britain and Afghanistan. **1839** Opium War: China and Britain. **1842** China hands over Hong Kong to Britain. **1842** Khyber Pass massacre of British forces by Afghans. **1845** War between British and Sikhs in India. **1850** Taiping rebellion, China. **1854** Japan signs a trade treaty with the USA. **1856–60** Britain and China at war again. **1857** Indian Mutiny; British crush uprising. **1860** British and French occupy Beijing. **1863** France 'protects' Cambodia – start of French empire in Indo-China.	**1818** Chaka founds Zulu empire. **1822** Liberia founded as colony for freed slaves. **1824** War between Britain and Ashanti kingdom (modern Ghana). **1830** Algeria becomes French colony. **1835** Great Trek begins, as Boer (Dutch) settlers move north from Cape into Transvaal. **1838** Boers defeat Zulus at Battle of Blood River. **1841** Muhammad Ali is declared ruler of Egypt. **1843** British defeat Boers, make Natal a crown colony. **1846** Xhosas fight Dutch and British in Cape Colony. **1851** British take Lagos, in Nigeria. **1852** Britain recognizes independence of Transvaal. **1852** Scottish missionary-explorer David Livingstone sets out on first of three great journeys across Africa (1852–6, 1858–63, 1866–71). **1862** John Speke discovers that River Nile source is Lake Victoria.	**1817** Bolivar forms an independent government in Venezuela. **1819** USA gains Florida from Spain. **1821** Mexico and Peru gain independence. **1822** Brazil independent. **1828** Uruguay independent. **1829** Greater Colombia split into four new states: Colmbia, Ecuador, New Granada and Venezuela. **1836** Texas wins independence from Mexico. **1838** Foundation of Central American republics. **1840** Act of Union in Canada: Upper and Lower Canada joined. **1846–8** War between USA and Mexico. USA gains California and New Mexico. **1848** Californian gold rush. **1859** First US oil well, in Pennsylvania. **1861** Start of American Civil War. **1863** President Lincoln frees the slaves. **1865** End of Civil War. South surrenders. Lincoln is murdered by John Wilkes Booth.

Last stand at the Alamo

⊙ THE ALAMO

Built as a Catholic mission in about 1718, the Alamo stands in San Antonio, Texas, USA. Until 1836 Texas was part of Mexico, but the many American settlers there rose against the Mexican dictator, Santa Anna. When San Antonio fell to the rebels, 5,000 Mexicans marched on the city. The Texans (under 200 men) withdrew to the Alamo and defended it for 12 days – enabling their army to regroup and, six weeks later, win independence. The heroes of the Alamo all died, among them the frontiersmen Jim Bowie and Davy Crockett.

The USA expands

The economic power of the United States was rapidly matching that of Europe. The country was growing fast, by spreading westward (see page 21). The Plains Indians were driven off their hunting grounds by ranchers and gold-prospectors, and the buffalo herds on which the Indians depended for food and clothing were slaughtered.

Many new settlers in America were Irish, fleeing a terrible famine in their homeland. Eastern cities were growing. Frontier posts like Chicago were becoming cities. In the south, the Texans fought for freedom from Mexico (see left) but they soon joined the United States. By 1850, the USA stretched from the Atlantic to the Pacific. Cattle raised on huge western ranches were shipped east by the new coast-to-coast railways.

PACIFIC

1825 Revolt in Java put down by Dutch.
1828 Colony of Western Australia founded.
1834 Colony of South Australia founded.
1839 British begin to settle in New Zealand.
1840 New Zealand becomes a British crown colony by treaty of Waitangi.
1845 The Maoris rebel against British settlers.
1850 Australian colonies granted responsible government.
1851 Gold rush in Australia.
1860 Second Maori War in New Zealand. Gold-seekers from abroad join New Zealand's gold rush.
1861 Women in Australia get the vote.

▶ KING COAL, KING COTTON

In the new age of mass production – making goods by machines in factories – millions of people became factory workers. The steam engines that drove the machines were fuelled by coal. Europe already had many coal mines, and mining in the United States developed rapidly during the 19th century. Deep down, men, women and children hauled heavy wheeled tubs of coal through dark, damp underground tunnels. In cotton mills too, women and children worked with machinery alongside men. Cotton grown in the Southern states of America was sold to the mills, to be spun into thread and woven into cloth.

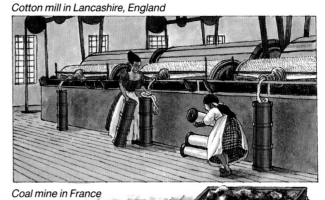
Cotton mill in Lancashire, England

Coal mine in France

Trade and colonization in Asia

In 1818 the British East India Company sent a young official, Stamford Raffles, to investigate a swampy island near Malaya called Singapura. Raffles saw possibilities and bought the island from the Malayan sultan. By 1821 its population had risen from 150 to 10,000. This was the beginning of the astonishing growth of the island, which, as Singapore, became one of Asia's great ports and trade centres.

China, once a mighty power, was now too weak to keep out foreigners. It refused to buy European goods, but corrupt officials let British merchants import opium. When the Chinese tried to end the opium trade, the British made war (see below). Subsequently, Chinese ports, including Shanghai, were opened to foreign trade for the first time. The Chinese economy underwent great change, as factories were set up. In the countryside, hungry peasants rose in revolt. The Taiping rebellion cost 20 million lives. Many poor Chinese went abroad to work as 'coolies' (labourers) in the Caribbean, Canada and the United States.

China was also under pressure from Russia, which was colonizing parts of central Asia, such as Kazakhstan. Russia seized Chinese territory bordering Korea and built a new Pacific port at Vladivostok. The French arrived in South-East Asia (Vietnam, Cambodia, Laos) to colonize the region.

Britain gradually extended its control over all the Indian subcontinent. British rule was briefly challenged in 1857 by an uprising known in Britain as the Indian Mutiny. This began as a protest by Indian soldiers but became a nationalist revolt, calling for a return to the glories of Mogul India.

British military power soon overcame the rebels, and the British government decided it was time to take over the running of India from the East India Company. India was to be the show-piece of the British Empire – the 'jewel in the imperial crown'.

▼ CHINA'S OPIUM WARS

Opium (a drug producing a trance-like state) was much used in China, even though it had been banned since 1729. The drug was imported by British traders. In 1839 the Chinese government seized all the opium in British-run warehouses, and war broke out between the countries. Though outnumbered, the British with modern ships and guns soon defeated the Chinese and made them sign a treaty opening five ports to British merchants. France joined Britain in a second Opium War from 1856 to 1860.

An opium den

▼ IN THE CRIMEA

In 1853 a Russian–Turkish dispute led to three years of war in the Crimean Peninsula, on the Black Sea. Britain and France joined Turkey, to stop Russia moving its navy into the Mediterranean. After victories by the allies at Balaklava (where the Light Brigade charged to fame) and Inkerman, came the siege of Sevastopol, during which thousands of troops died from cold and disease. Florence Nightingale's nursing saved thousands more, and her reports back to Britain led to reforms being made in the army and in nursing.

Nursing in the Crimea

⊙ THE GROWTH OF AMERICA

Between 1789 and 1854 the number of states of the USA grew from 13 to 31. The new states mapped a rapid movement of settlement westward: Illinois 1818, Iowa 1846, Nebraska 1867. In the south, Texas freed itself from Mexico and became a state in 1845. The enormous western territories of Oregon, gained from joint British rule in 1846, and California, from Mexico in 1848, almost completed the mainland jigsaw. The population rose from 3 million in the 1780s to 22 million in the 1840s, reaching almost 40 million by the end of the 1860s. Ships brought new settlers from Europe. Many came with only their clothes and a bag of belongings, to work in factories, or to farm the land. Many were also escaping from hunger or persecution.

△ Immigrants crossed the Atlantic by ship. Few had many possessions; they went to North America with little else but hope.

US EXPANSION

1819 Florida becomes part of USA.
1820 US states number 22.
1835 Erie Canal opens new shipping route from Atlantic to Great Lakes.
1834 McCormick's new mechanical reaper speeds up farmers' grain harvests.
1840s Wagon trains cross the Great Plains. Most Indians driven west of Mississippi.
1848 USA wins war with Mexico, gains more land. California gold rush.
1850 California becomes a state.
1861–5 Civil War between North and South; North's victory ends slavery and stops South becoming a separate country. Number of US states 36.

▽ Many pioneers who settled the American West built their own homes. Often a timber and turf cabin was a family's first home. In 1848, thousands of people rushed to California, hoping to find gold. Only a lucky few made their fortunes.

Miners panning for gold

Garibaldi, Italy's hero

Japan and the Pacific

Japan had little contact with foreigners, but it was by no means backward. Its education system was good, with schools in many villages. But the arrival of a US naval mission in 1853 (see below) still came as a cultural shock. The generals, or shoguns, who ruled Japan knew they lagged behind the West in technology. Reluctantly, they were forced to allow Western traders into Japan.

Australia was explored gradually. Its interior was mostly desert, but in 1851 gold was discovered. When the diggers (miners) rebelled in 1854 at Eureka, Victoria, it was a landmark on the road to democracy in Australia. The oldest colonies – New South Wales, Victoria, Tasmania and South Australia – were granted self-government in 1856.

In New Zealand the warlike Maoris fought among themselves and against the European settlers, but by 1840 New Zealand was a British colony. Europeans brought Christianity and new foods such as potatoes.

⊙ JAPAN MEETS THE WEST

On 8 July 1853, US Navy ships entered Tokyo Bay, in Japan. The squadron's commander was Matthew Calbraith Perry. For two centuries the Japanese had cut themselves off from all contacts with Europe and America. Japanese life had hardly changed in that time, and Japan's rulers had shunned foreign trade. Perry had come to change their minds, by force if necessary. When Perry returned home in 1854, he had what he wanted: a treaty allowing the USA to trade with Japan through two ports.

US envoy Perry in Japan

⊛ GARIBALDI UNITES ITALY

Giuseppe Garibaldi was born in Nice in 1807. In the 1830s he fought in South America; in 1848 he fought for freedom in Italy. For a time, Garibaldi lived in the United States, before returning in 1854 to farm on an island near Sardinia. In 1859 another war began with the aim to free and unite the states of Italy. Garibaldi left home to lead an army of 1,000 'redshirt' volunteers to victory. Italy was united in 1861, under King Victor Emmanuel of Piedmont–Sardinia. Garibaldi refused all honours and retired to his farm.

The slave question

Slavery, an old evil, was still a worldwide problem. Britain had banned the slave trade in its colonies, and the British navy hunted down slave ships. Africa remained the centre of the slave trade, as it had been since the 1500s. The British missionary–explorer David Livingstone journeyed across Africa, to expose the evils of slavery. In West Africa a new country named Liberia was founded as a homeland for freed slaves from America.

The issue of slavery divided the United States. The Northern states, which had most of the nation's factories, did not have slaves. In the South, cotton and tobacco planters relied on their black slave workers. Many Northerners wanted to put an end to slavery, but the South rejected any interference in its affairs. The North–South quarrel became a civil war (see page 23).

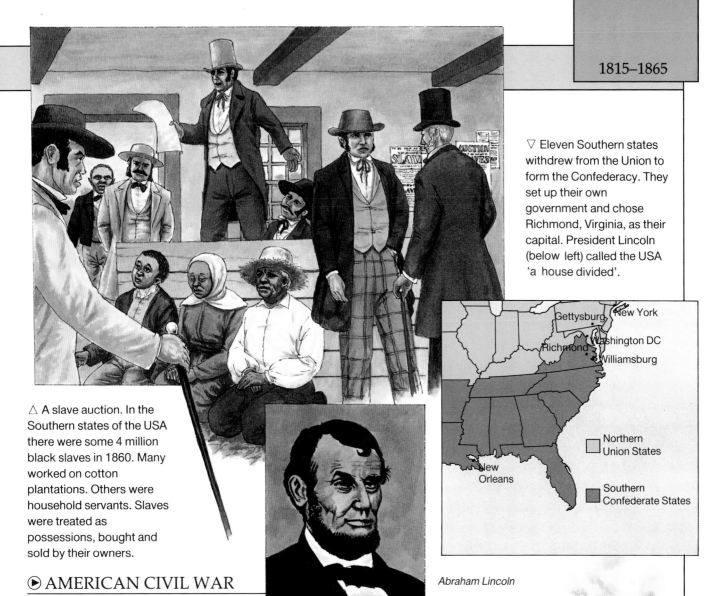

▽ Eleven Southern states withdrew from the Union to form the Confederacy. They set up their own government and chose Richmond, Virginia, as their capital. President Lincoln (below left) called the USA 'a house divided'.

Northern Union States

Southern Confederate States

△ A slave auction. In the Southern states of the USA there were some 4 million black slaves in 1860. Many worked on cotton plantations. Others were household servants. Slaves were treated as possessions, bought and sold by their owners.

Abraham Lincoln

⊙ AMERICAN CIVIL WAR

In 1861 the 11 slave-states of the Southern United States formed a Confederacy and broke away from the rest of the Union. President Abraham Lincoln refused to let the USA become two nations, and civil war began in April 1861. The South elected its own President, Jefferson Davis, and formed an army led by experienced soldiers such as General Robert E. Lee. However, the Northern industrial states had more men, more money, more railways, and more warships. The North won a key victory at Gettysburg (Virginia) in 1863, the year in which Lincoln declared all black slaves to be free. Many blacks joined the Northern armies. Union generals Ulysses S. Grant and William Tecumseh Sherman split the Southern forces, and in April 1865 General Lee surrendered. The war, which cost 600,000 lives, permanently reunited the country but left the South in ruins.

▷ Confederate prisoners of war guarded by Union troops after one of the many Civil War battles. The Northerners ('Yankees') outnumbered the Southerners ('Rebs'), and had more resources.

19TH-CENTURY CITY

▽ Rebuilding a European city. As cities grew, their suburbs spread into the surrounding countryside. Railway lines were built to carry passengers into the city centre. Many old streets were demolished. Workers' houses were usually crammed close together, for cheapness. Many such poorly designed homes soon became slums.

By the 1800s, cities in Europe and America, and in Asia, were growing so fast that old-fashioned city governments could no longer cope. There were simply too many people moving to the cities. The newcomers crowded into ramshackle slums consisting of small cramped houses or hastily built apartment blocks, with poor sanitation.

Planning the new cities

Because cities lacked drains and clean drinking water, outbreaks of disease such as typhus and cholera were common. Cities needed firefighters, police, hospitals, schools, street-cleaners and rubbish collectors. In the past, these services had been provided only in a haphazard way.

In the mid-1800s city governments began to tackle the problems seriously. They started police and fire departments, schools and hospitals. They dug sewers and laid pipes to carry clean drinking water. Engineers built railways and roads, knocking down old wooden houses and replacing them with steel and brick.

△ A bustling square in Munich, Germany. Cars have not yet displaced horses and handcarts. Trams running on rails provide public transport.

▽ Montmartre in Paris, by the Impressionist painter Camille Pissarro. Paris, replanned in the 1850s, was a favourite city for artists and writers.

CITY GROWTH

1820 New York has 124,000 people; London over 1 million.
1822 Boston and other US cities elect mayors.
1828–9 Horse-drawn buses in Paris and London.
1830s Gas lighting in most large cities.
1835 Fire destroys most of old New York.
1850 New York's population tops 500,000.
1850s Paris (population over 1 million) rebuilt by Haussman, with wide roads and squares.
1850s London's water, drains and sewers improved.
1856 New York buys Central Park.
1863 First underground railway, London.

GREAT POWER RIVALRY

By the 1860s the most powerful nations were able to enforce their will almost anywhere in the world. Britain had the strongest navy; its iron-clad warships steamed across the oceans, defending and enlarging an already huge empire. The United States was growing stronger, too, and began to extend its power in the Pacific.

In Europe, Germany was united by 1871. Otto von Bismarck, chief minister of Prussia from 1862, achieved this by making allies of the smaller German states in short wars against Austria and France (see page 27).

A changing map

Nations strove for supremacy by making alliances to alter the 'balance of power'. Russia conquered more land in Asia and seized large chunks of China. Italy completed its unification.

In eastern Europe, Turkey faced nationalist revolts in its subject states of the Balkans. Russia claimed to be the champion of all Slav peoples and fought against Turkey. Serbia, Montenegro and Albania gained independence from the Turks in 1878. But the 'Balkan question' of who owned which areas remained largely unresolved.

New links between East and West

The world was shrinking, as steamships replaced slower sailing vessels, and the Suez Canal shortened the sea journey from Europe to Asia (see below). Imperial powers needed such sea routes to protect their Asian territories. Britain had India, France had Indo-China, and the Dutch ruled the East Indies. Elsewhere in Asia, Japan was fast becoming a modern nation (see page 27).

An age of steel

Iron and steel were the framework of this new world. Steel was used to make railway tracks, ships, bridges – and buildings. High above Paris rose a startling new landmark, the Eiffel Tower, built in 1889 to celebrate the centenary of the French Revolution.

▼ THE SUEZ CANAL OPENS

The Suez Canal, one of the engineering feats of the 1800s, was planned by the French engineer Ferdinand de Lesseps. It linked the Mediterranean and Red Seas, crossing almost 124 miles of Egyptian desert. Work began in 1859, and the Canal was opened by a procession of ships in November 1869. Britain had opposed the building of the Canal, but soon realized its importance as a short cut to the East for trade and warships. In 1875 the British government bought shares in the Canal from the ruler of Egypt.

The opening of the Suez Canal

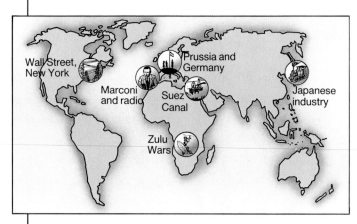

△ The Suez Canal speeded up travel from Europe to Asia, cutting out the voyage around Africa. Britain, France, Germany and Russia ruled empires. Japan was modernizing, but China was weakening.

1865–1880	1880 – 1900
1866 Prussia defeats Austria. **1867** USA buys Alaska from Russia. **1869** Suez Canal is opened. **1870** Italian unification complete; Rome becomes national capital. **1870** Franco–Prussian War. France defeated. **1871** German Empire proclaimed. **1871** Paris Commune (uprising) crushed. **1874** First exhibition of Impressionist paintings, Paris. **1876** Telephone invented, by Scotsman Alexander Graham Bell in the USA. **1876** Battle of Little Bighorn (USA); Sioux Indians defeat Custer's cavalry. **1877** Queen Victoria made Empress of India. **1878** Treaty of Berlin attempts to solve Balkans' problems. **1879–80** Wars in Southern Africa, involving British, Boers and Zulus.	**1881** Boers fight British in South Africa. **1883** Boer leader Kruger becomes President of Transvaal. **1884** Berlin Conference, European nations scramble to seize colonies in Africa. **1885** Indian National Congress meets for first time. **1885** Sudanese rebels capture Khartoum. **1885** First motor car, built by Karl Benz (Germany). **1890** Massacre of Indians at Wounded Knee, USA. **1893** USA annexes Hawaii. **1894** Scandal over conviction of Captain Dreyfus, a Jew, for spying (France). **1895** End of war between China and Japan: Japanese power growing. **1898** Spanish–American War, won by USA. **1898** Britain and France clash in Sudan. **1899** Boer War starts in South Africa.

New technology made possible more terrible weapons: powerful explosives, huge cannons, rifles and machine guns. Whole armies could be moved swiftly by rail and steamer. Wars became bloodier, with much greater loss of life.

The United States and Canada

After the Civil War, the United States underwent a period of growth and change. The South recovered slowly from the war. Blacks were now free citizens, but few were treated as equals to whites. The Indians fought their last battles for their territory against the US Army. Their fate was sealed in 1869, when the first transcontinental railway was completed, linking East and West and opening the way for more white settlers.

▼ A NEW ERA IN JAPAN

After 1853 Japan was 'open' to the outside world. Many Japanese felt humiliated by the unfair treaties their government had signed with the USA and European powers. In 1867 a group of nobles rebelled; they forced the ruling shogun to resign and restored power to the emperor, a 16-year-old. The capital was moved from Kyoto to Edo (which was renamed Tokyo), and the emperor took the name Meiji. During his reign (1867–1912) Japan modernized itself into a strong industrial and military nation.

Japan's first railway, 1872

▼ PRUSSIA DEFEATS FRANCE

In 1870 Prussia's Chancellor, Otto von Bismarck, manoeuvred the French into a brief, bloody war against Prussia and its German allies. At the battle of Sedan, Prussian guns destroyed the French army. Emperor Napoleon III fled to Britain, and France became a republic. Then, for months, Paris was besieged while revolutionaries fought for a socialist Commune. In 1871, at France's Versailles Palace, Prussia's king was proclaimed Emperor of all Germany.

The Prussian siege of Paris

While American farmers ploughed the prairies, US industry boomed. The country was getting rich, and a fortunate few businessmen became millionaires and household names – men like Andrew Carnegie (from steel) and John D Rockefeller (oil). In 1867 the United States bought from Russia the huge northwestern territory of Alaska. In 1893 it took over Hawaii.

Every immigrant ship docking in New York brought more new Americans (see pages 19, 21, 29). Among them were Italians and Irish, Swedes and Germans. Others were refugees from Russia and countries in eastern Europe.

Canada, to the north, was still thinly settled, compared to the United States. In 1867 English-speaking and French-speaking Canada were united in one self-governing Dominion, as part of the British Empire.

Central and South America

When, in 1895, Cuba revolted against Spain, the United States aided the rebels, and afterwards effectively controlled Cuba. The small and poor Central American republics were largely ignored, but the Americans were interested in building a canal across the Isthmus of Panama to link the Atlantic and Pacific oceans. The French started to dig a canal in the 1880s, but lack of money and disease forced them to give up.

The republics of South America were ruled by a succession of dictators, usually generals and rich landowners. Slaves were freed, but most people still lived in poverty as peasant farmers. There were violent border disputes. In the 1860s Argentina, Brazil and Uruguay joined forces to defeat Paraguay. In the 1880s Chile defeated Bolivia and Peru and deprived Bolivia of its sea coast.

EUROPE	ASIA	AFRICA	AMERICA
1866 Austria and Prussia at war. **1866** Italy gains Venice. **1867** Austro-Hungarian dual monarchy; Franz Josef of Austria becomes King of Hungary. **1870** Italy annexes Rome, which in 1871 becomes Italy's capital. **1870–1** War between France and Prussia. **1871** Germany is united under Emperor Wilhelm I. **1871** Third French Republic. Paris Commune crushed. **1876** Bulgarians revolt against Turks, but fail. Turkey defeats Serbia. **1877** Russia and Turkey at war over the Balkans. **1878** Congress of Berlin. Britain, Germany and Austria try to reduce Russia's influence in the Balkans. **1878** Treaty of San Stefano: Montenegro, Serbia, Bulgaria and Romania free from Turkey. **1886** Irish Home Rule Bill defeated in British Parliament. **1890** Bismarck loses power in Germany.	**1867** End of shogun rule in Japan, start of Meiji modernization period. **1877** Queen Victoria declared Empress of India. **1885** First meeting of Indian National Congress. **1885** France gains protectorates over Annam and Tonkin (Indo-China). Britain occupies part of Burma. **1891** Russians start building the Trans-Siberian Railway. **1894** Japan and China at war. **1895** Treaty of Shimonoseki ends China–Japan war. Japan victorious, gains Formosa (Taiwan). Korea independent, but Japanese-controlled. **1896** Britain and France agree territorial limits in Siam (Thailand). **1898** China hands Port Arthur to Russia. **1900** Rebellion in China by the 'Society of Harmonious Fists', or Boxers. Europeans are attacked.	**1866** Livingstone starts his third great exploration of central Africa. **1869** Suez Canal opened. **1873** Second war between Ashanti and Britain in Gold Coast **1875** Britain gains control of Suez Canal. **1879** Zulu wars in southern Africa; Zulus defeated by British. **1880** Revolt by Boers in South Africa. Transvaal independent. **1881** France occupies Tunisia, in North Africa. **1884** Berlin Conference; European powers share out Africa. **1885** War in Sudan. Khartoum falls to the Mahdi's army. General Gordon killed. **1889** Italy makes Ethiopia a protectorate. **1890** Cecil Rhodes founds Rhodesia. **1893** France colonizes Ivory Coast in West Africa. **1898** Fashoda 'incident', crisis between Britain and France in Sudan. Britain and Egypt defeat Sudanese rebels. **1899** Boer War begins in South Africa.	**1866** First US civil rights law to safeguard black citizens. **1867** USA buys Alaska from Russia. **1867** Canada becomes a Dominion. **1869** First railway across the USA completed. **1870** Manitoba becomes part of Canada, as does British Columbia (1871). **1873** North-West Mounted Police founded in Canada. **1876** Last Indian victory over US Cavalry, at Little Bighorn. **1879** War of the Pacific in South America: Chile defeats Bolivia and Peru. **1881** US President Garfield is assassinated. **1885** Canadian Pacific Railway completed. **1889** Brazil becomes a republic. **1890** Massacre of Wounded Knee, the last defeat of the Plains Indians. **1893** USA annexes Hawaii. **1898** Spanish–American War. USA gains Puerto Rico, Guam, Philippines. Cuba independent.

New York street in 1892

⦿ NEW YORK BOOMS

As their ships approached New York harbour, many immigrants caught their first glimpse of the United States in the shape of the Statue of Liberty – a gift from France in 1884 – welcoming new arrivals. New York in the late 1800s was a booming city. Its financial district, Wall Street, was the business centre of the country. Its port was the biggest in America. Its streets teemed with people from many countries, speaking many different languages.

Power politics

The strong nations did more or less as they liked. They shared out Africa (see pages 30–31). Their guns defeated local resistance, even from the warlike Zulus (see below).

In 1877, the British declared their queen, Victoria, Empress of India. British India seemed unshakeable. Yet there were stirrings of protest. The National Congress Party was formed to campaign for a free India.

Inventions and women's rights

Developments in transport and communications included the motor car, electric light bulb, telephone, phonograph and tape recorder. Radio and moving pictures were soon to follow (see below centre). Meanwhile women gained new job opportunities in office work through the use of the typewriter (an 1860s invention).

PACISIC

1867 New Zealand for the first time has more Europeans (200,000) than Maoris.
1867 End of transportation (shipment of convicts to Australia).
1870s Dutch now control all East Indies (Indonesia).
1872 First telegraph linking Australia with outside world.
1872 End of the Maori wars in New Zealand.
1874 Fiji becomes a British colony.
1879 First Indian sugar-workers arrive in Fiji.
1880 Ned Kelly, Australian bushranger (bandit) executed.
1880s Railway boom in Australia.
1882 First shipment of refrigerated food from New Zealand to Britain.
1885 Germany and Britain share New Guinea between them.
1890s Economic slump and strikes in Australia.
1893 Women gain the vote in New Zealand.
1896 Philippines break from Spanish rule.
1899 USA gains control of Philippines.

⦿ MARCONI

Guglielmo Marconi, an Italian, did most to bring about the modern miracle of radio. In 1895 he sent the first telegraph signals through the air (instead of along wires). He went to work in Britain and, by 1901, had so improved his 'wireless' system that he sent the first wireless telegraph message in Morse code across the Atlantic Ocean.

Marconi's 'wireless'

Zulus fighting for their land

⦿ THE ZULU WARS

The Zulu people of southern Africa carved out an empire in the 1800s, led by their warrior-kings Dingiswayo, Chaka and Cetewayo. The Zulus' formidable armies fought to hold their land against both the Boers (Dutch) and the British. They were finally overcome by the British army in 1879. Zululand eventually became part of British Natal.

CARVING UP AFRICA

Before 1850, few white people had explored Africa beyond the coast. Inland, there were no roads or railways. Travellers faced danger from disease, wild animals and warring tribes. Journeys by white explorers, such as Richard Burton, John Hanning Speke, David Livingstone and Henry Morton Stanley, revealed the vastness of Africa and inspired others.

The unknown continent

To Europeans and Americans, most of Africa was the 'Dark Continent', and 'uncivilized'. They knew of Egypt's long history, and of Ethiopia's proud independence. But they knew little of Africa's Muslim empires, or of the flourishing kingdoms in West and Central Africa. African culture was not understood, only domination. Western power made it easy for the king of Belgium to take over an enormous area of the Congo in 1885 and to rule it harshly as his personal 'estate'.

▽ David Livingstone's map-making kit. This Scottish missionary-explorer (1813–73) spent 30 years in Africa. His journeys, on foot, helped fill in many gaps in African geography. Livingstone was determined to end the slave trade. Unlike some other European travellers, he respected the African people and their ways.

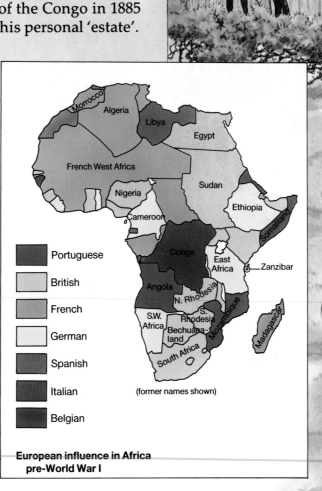

Portuguese

British

French

German

Spanish

Italian

Belgian

Morrocco
Algeria
Libya
Egypt
French West Africa
Nigeria
Sudan
Cameroon
Ethiopia
Somaliland
Congo
East Africa
Zanzibar
Angola
N. Rhodesia
S.W. Africa
S. Rhodesia
Mozambique
Bechuana-land
Madagascar
South Africa

(former names shown)

European influence in Africa pre-World War I

Yoruba carving, Nigeria

◁ A Dogon village in Mali (once an empire, but a French colony in the 1800s). Few Europeans understood African culture, although they admired some African art and warrior–peoples like the Zulus. Christian missionaries tried to convert Africans from their traditional religions.

◁ Visitors arrive at a colonial outpost. European officials went to Africa, as did traders, engineers, teachers, doctors and missionaries. A few African rulers made agreements with the Europeans and thereby kept some of their former power.

POWER IN AFRICA

1866 David Livingstone sets out from Zanzibar into central Africa.
1869 Suez Canal opened.
1860s Muslim empires rule most of western Africa; France and Belgium seize colonies.
1870s Diamonds and gold found in South Africa.
1871 Stanley and Livingstone meet at Ujiji, near Lake Tanganyika.
1873 Slave market at Zanzibar closes.
1877 Britain annexes Transvaal.
1879 British defeat Zulus.
1880s Britain controls Egypt.
1883 Paul Kruger President of South African Republic.
1884 Berlin Conference: Europe shares out Africa.
1885 War in Sudan. Italy claims Eritrea.
1890 Cecil Rhodes founds Rhodesia.
1896 Ethiopians defeat Italians at Adowa.
1899 Boer War begins in South Africa.

Britain's Cecil Rhodes (1853–1902) and other empire-builders dreamed of building a railway from Cairo in Egypt to the Cape of Good Hope at Africa's southern tip. They wanted to settle Africa, as America had been settled. In fact, much of Africa was unsuitable for European-style farming, but there were riches: gold and diamonds, timber and tropical crops such as cocoa.

By 1900 most Africans were ruled by Europeans. France and Spain had colonized much of North Africa. Egypt and the Sudan were under British control. France and Belgium had large colonies in the west; Germany, Britain and Portugal held much of the east. Britain's empire included most of southern Africa, where the British army fought the Zulus and the Boers (see page 29). The Boers were the longest-rooted white settlers in Africa, and they fought fiercely but in vain for their independence.

31

WAR AND ITS AFTERMATH

As the 20th century began, Europe was a giant arms factory, producing weapons for a new war. Two old enemies, Britain and France, were allies against the growing strength of Germany. In Russia, revolution was in the offing. The Russian tsar, aloof from his people, still ruled his crumbling empire like a medieval kingdom.

There was revolution too in Asia, where the Chinese empire was unable to adjust to the modern world. China's ancient throne tottered. In 1905 Japan, which had modernized rapidly since the 1860s (see page 27), won an astonishing victory in a war against imperial Russia.

Across the Pacific, the United States took no part in foreign quarrels. The US government was concerned mainly with the Americas – Mexico, Panama and South America. With vast natural resources and a growing population, the United States was fast becoming the world's richest nation.

With the new century came the invention of the aeroplane (see right). Mastery of the air brought a new era of travel, as well as a new and terrifying weapon of war.

The first powered aeroplane flight

◉ THE WRIGHTS FLY INTO HISTORY

On 17 December 1903, six people watched history being made at Kitty Hawk in North Carolina, USA. On its lonely sandhills, Wilbur and Orville Wright prepared their latest flying machine, the *Flyer I*. It was Orville's turn to be pilot, lying on his stomach. The small home-made petrol engine roared, the twin propellers whirled, and the first aeroplane rose into the air – travelling just 121 feet. By 1908 the Wright brothers were making flights of 2½ hours. Other aviators followed where they had led.

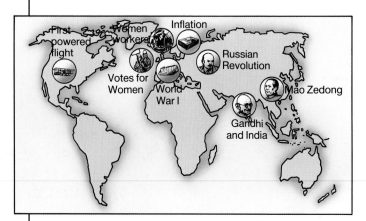

△ The First World War was fought mostly in Europe. The Austro-Hungarian and Turkish empires broke up. The USA helped win the war but tried to retreat into isolation in the 1930s. Then a second world war threatened. Dictators ruled Italy, Germany and the USSR. There was civil war in Spain and China.

1900–1920

1901 Australia becomes a united federal commonwealth.
1902 Boer War ends in South Africa.
1903 Orville and Wilbur Wright make first aeroplane flights.
1904–5 Japan defeats Russia in war.
1910 Formation of Union of South Africa.
1911 Revolution in China, which becomes a republic.
1914 Panama Canal opens to shipping.
1914 Outbreak of World War I. Central powers – Germany, Austria, Turkey and allies – at war with France, Britain, Russia, Italy, Japan and, from 1917, the USA.
1917 Revolutions in Russia in March and November.
1918 World War I ends.
1919 Britons Alcock and Brown fly the Atlantic.
1919 Upsurge of nationalist protest against British rule in India.
1920 USA refuses to ratify Paris peace treaties to end World War I and withdraws into isolation.

1920–1939

1920 League of Nations set up as peace-keeping organization.
1920s Chaos in Germany; weak government, collapsing economy.
1920s Radio broadcasting begins.
1920s Prohibition (of alcohol) in USA.
1924 Death of Lenin, Russian revolutionary leader.
1927 Civil war in China.
1927 First talking pictures.
1929 Financial collapse in USA, spreads worldwide. Mass unemployment hits industrialized countries.
1933 New Deal policy in USA.
1933 Hitler becomes leader of Germany.
1934 Long March of Chinese Communists.
1936–9 Civil War in Spain.
1937 Japan attacks China. Japan makes an alliance with Germany and Italy.
1938 Germany seizes Austria, threatens Czechoslovakia (occupied 1939).
1939 Germany invades Poland. World War II begins.

The First World War

The war in Europe that began in 1914 was the worst in history (see below). It was sparked off by disputes in central Europe, where old empires were falling apart and new nations were striving for independence. Germany joined Austria–Hungary and Turkey to fight Britain, France, Russia and Italy. The fighting spread to the Middle East.

▶ THE 'GREAT WAR'

This 'war to end wars' was fought with new and terrible weapons by the huge opposing armies. Millions of soldiers at the 'Front' lived and died in mazes of trenches and barbed wire, bombarded by gunfire that blasted fields and forests into cratered wastelands. Aeroplanes and airships dropped bombs from the skies; submarines stalked merchant ships at sea. Tanks trundled through the mud, spitting fire from their machine-guns. Clouds of poison gas drifted silently on the breeze. Each attack, to win a few metres of ground, cost thousands of lives.

While the navies of Britain and Germany met only once, at the battle of Jutland, their armies faced each other across a vast muddy battleground of trenches. Generals still fought by the old rules, ordering suicidal charges by infantry against enemy artillery. Civilians suffered too, from aerial bombardment. Some 10 million people were killed in the war, with over twice as many wounded.

▷ The land and air battles were fought mostly in Europe, where millions of soldiers manned trenches.

German advance into France, Sept. 1914

WORLD WAR I

1914 Germany invades Belgium and France.
1915 Allies attack Turks at Gallipoli. Italy fights Austria–Hungary. First gas attacks by Germans.
1916 Naval battle of Jutland. Land battle of the Somme.
1917 USA enters war. Russian Revolution. Russia pulls out of the war (1918).
1918 Last German attack fails. Armistice (11 November) ends the war.

◁ British battleships protected convoys carrying supplies to Britain from the Empire and the USA.

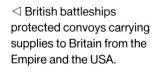

▽ Soldiers going 'over the top'. During such attacks, thousands died amid the mud and barbed wire.

The Great War, as people called it, exhausted Europe. The United States joined the conflict in 1917, adding its fresh forces and industrial might to aid Britain and France. Soon afterwards, Russia was on the point of defeat by Germany, and faced revolution at home (see page 35).

By end-1918 Germany itself was near collapse and sued for peace. The German emperor was forced to abdicate, and the guns stopped firing. But the Peace of Versailles, which formally concluded the war, did not bring about long-term stability in Europe.

The world of the 1920s was very different from the way it had been before 1914. The Great War had redrawn territories and changed people's lives. In particular, women were able to find new work and pursue new ambitions (see right).

▼ WOMEN AT WORK

The change in women's lives from working on the farm, or at home in 'cottage' industries, to working in mines and factories began in the 1800s. During World War I, so many men were away in the army that women of all social groups were recruited to do men's work, for example as bus drivers and office workers. When peace returned, many women went back to home life, but with the spread of birth control, more could choose an independent career.

Woman factory worker

EUROPE	ASIA	AFRICA	AMERICA
1905 Russia defeated by Japan. **1905** Failed revolution in Russia; some reforms. **1912–13** Balkan Wars. **1914** World War I begins. **1916** Battles of Somme (land) and Jutland (sea). **1916** Easter Rising in Ireland. **1917** Russian Revolution overthrows tsar. **1918** World War I ends. **1918–21** Civil war in Russia. **1919** Treaty of Versailles. League of Nations founded (1920). **1921** Irish Free State is set up. **1922** Mussolini, Fascist leader, heads new government in Italy. **1924** Death of Lenin. **1926** General strike in Britain. **1933** Hitler becomes head of German government. **1936** Abdication of Britain's King Edward VIII. **1936** Civil war in Spain. **1936** Germany occupies the Rhineland. **1938** Munich crisis. **1939** Germany attacks Poland. Britain and France declare war on Germany.	**1904–5** War between Japan and Russia. Japan wins. **1910** Japan takes over Korea. **1911** Revolution in China; new republic led by Sun Yat-sen. **1914–18** World War I. Japan joins Allies. Arabs revolt against Turks. **1917** Balfour Declaration promises the Jews a homeland in Palestine. **1919** Unrest in India. Gandhi leads passive resistance movement. **1920** France given mandate to rule Syria and Lebanon. Britain made responsible for Iraq, Palestine, Transjordan. **1921** Reza Khan seizes power in Persia, becomes Shah (emperor) in 1925. **1922** Last Sultan of Ottoman Turkey deposed. **1923** Turkey a republic. **1927** Civil War in China between Communists and Nationalists. **1931** Japanese occupy Manchuria. **1932** Kingdom of Saudi Arabia created. **1934** Communists begin Long March in China.	**1902** Boer War ends in South Africa. **1907** Belgian government takes over Congo colony, from King Leopold III. **1910** South Africa becomes an independent Dominion. **1911** Italy conquers Libya. **1911** Agadir crisis: France forced to hand over territory in Morocco to Germany. **1912** France controls Morocco. **1914** World War I; French and British fight for German colonies. **1920** After World War I, Britain is granted a mandate over ex-German East Africa. Kenya becomes a British colony. **1922** Egypt becomes self-governing. **1925** Uprising in Morocco put down by France and Spain. **1930** Haile Selassie, last emperor of Ethiopia, crowned. **1935** Italy invades Ethiopia, to make it a colony.	**1901** US President McKinley assassinated; Theodore Roosevelt succeeds him. **1903** Wright brothers make first flight. **1909** Peary and Henson reach North Pole. **1910** Civil War in Mexico. **1914** Opening of Panama Canal. **1917** USA declares war on Germany. **1919** President Woodrow Wilson helps set up the League of Nations. **1919** First flights across the Atlantic. **1920–33** Prohibition (ban on sale of alcoholic drinks) in USA. Leads to crime wave. **1929** Wall Street Crash; US stock market collapses, businesses ruined. Start of Great Depression (falling trade, unemployment). **1930** Military take-over in Brazil. Vargas becomes President. **1932** Chaco War, between Bolivia and Uruguay. **1933** Roosevelt's New Deal programme in the USA. **1939** USA declares it will stay neutral in World War II.

The world after the war

After its defeat, Germany became a republic. Its economy was wrecked, its money was worthless, its people were bitter. Germany was left with huge war debts and fines to pay. Its government was unpopular, and people began to listen to Adolf Hitler and the Nazi party (see pages 38–39).

Britain and France were no longer strong enough to rule their huge empires. In Africa and India, nationalists led campaigns for self-government (see page 36). The League of Nations was formed to prevent further wars, but this organization had no real power.

Russia rose from revolution and civil war as the Union of Soviet Socialist Republics (USSR), the world's first Communist state (see right). It was led by Lenin until his death in 1924, and later by Stalin.

ⓥ RUSSIAN REVOLUTION

The revolution that overwhelmed Russia in 1917 had been brewing for years. Strikes, peasant uprisings and mutinies in the army and navy had almost removed the weak tsar in 1905. In 1917 Russia was close to defeat by Germany and in chaos at home. Hungry workers in St Petersburg rioted in the streets, troops joined them, and in March Tsar Nicholas gave up his throne. A new government failed to improve things, and in November 1917 the Bolshevik (Marxist) leader Vladimir Ulyanov, known as Lenin, seized power. Russia's new Communist rulers arrested and later killed the tsar, took over all businesses, divided nobles' estates among the peasants, and pulled Russia out of the war.

The Bolshevik leader, Lenin

> Lenin (1870–1924) addresses a crowd during the Bolshevik Revolution. The tsar and his family (below) were held under house-arrest in Siberia and later executed.

PACIFIC

1901 Commonwealth of Australia established.
1911 New Zealand's population tops 1 million.
1912 First internal air services in Australia.
1914 Australia and New Zealand declare war on Germany.
Australian and New Zealand troops (Anzacs) join with British in World War I. German colonies in the Pacific taken over by Australia and New Zealand.
1920s Some 300,000 immigrants, mainly from Britain, enter Australia.
1926 Canberra becomes federal capital of Australia.
1928 Kingsford-Smith (Australia) flies from USA to Australia, across the Pacific Ocean.
1930s Australia and New Zealand suffer economic depression, as world trade slumps.
1934 First air service between Britain and Australia.
1935 New Zealand's first socialist government.
1939 Australia and New Zealand declare war on Germany.

⊽ VOTES FOR WOMEN

Until the early 1900s women in most countries had fewer legal rights than men: they could not vote in elections, or be elected to government. Reformers, such as Susan B Anthony in the USA and Emmeline Pankhurst in Britain, who campaigned for equality for all women, were known as 'suffragettes' (because they demonstrated publicly for women's suffrage, or voting rights). Some were sent to prison and badly treated. But, by the 1920s, women in a number of countries had won the right to vote.

Women could now vote

⊼ GANDHI'S INDIA

Gandhi in London, 1931

Mohandas Karamchand Gandhi led India's struggle for independence from British rule. He first fought for Indian rights as a lawyer in South Africa, using non-violent 'passive resistance'. In the 1920s and 1930s Gandhi used similar tactics in India. But when independence came, in 1947, it created two countries – India for Hindus and Pakistan for Muslims. Gandhi taught a simple lifestyle and was called 'Mahatma', or Great Soul. He was shot dead by a Hindu fanatic in 1948.

The Twenties and Thirties

After the Great War, the United States led the way into the 'Roaring Twenties' with all things modern: radio, records, movies, cars, refrigerators. American women had won the right to vote, as had most women in Europe (see above).

Britain struggled through a general strike in 1926. France was also weak. So was Russia, undergoing a massive reconstruction of farming and industry on state-run lines.

America catches a cold

The United States hoped to return to its pre-1917 isolation. Its main concerns were at home, and it wanted no more foreign wars. The future looked bright, as western states such as California flourished.

However, world trade and finance were now so interlinked that, when America had problems, the rest of the industrial world suffered too. In 1929 the US stock market collapsed. Banks and factories shut down. Investors lost their savings. So began the slump in world trade known as the Great Depression. Everywhere millions of industrial workers lost their jobs.

New Deal, new dictators

The Depression affected the whole world. In the United States the government of President Franklin Roosevelt launched a recovery programme known as the New Deal, funding projects to build irrigation schemes and dams. This helped to pull the country out of the slump, and during the 1930s life improved for many people (see page 37).

In Europe, there was no new deal, but a steady drift towards the unthinkable – a second Great War. Civil war in Spain between Fascists and Republicans proved to be a rehearsal for a new European war.

In Asia, China's Communists and Nationalists also fought a bitter civil war (see page 37). Divided and weakened, China presented a tempting target for Japan's military rulers, who dreamed of a greater Japanese empire.

△ Workers on the Ford car assembly line. America's factories led in modern production methods.

▷ Economic crisis in Germany in the 1930s; workers' wages could be trolley-loads of million-Deutschmark banknotes.

⊕ LIFE IN THE THIRTIES

The 1930s brought hard times for many people in the United States and Europe: there were soup kitchens to feed the hungry and protest marches by the jobless. To forget their troubles, people listened to the radio and went to the cinema; both were hugely popular. In the newspapers that brought them world news, they also read about Hollywood movie stars and record-breakers in the air, on land and on water. New inventions included frozen peas, nylon and the radio telescope. In 1935 the BBC in London started the world's first television service. A new US board game, Monopoly, was a hit in 1936. Sports events attracted large crowds. At the 1936 Olympic Games in Germany, the black US athlete Jesse Owens won four gold medals.

⊽ CHINA AND THE LONG MARCH

The Chinese republic, founded in 1912, was rocked by civil war after President Sun Yat-sen died in 1925. The Nationalists, led by Chiang Kai-shek, formed a government and, in 1927, began fighting the Communists. In 1934 Mao Zedong led about 100,000 Communists on the 'Long March' to the northern province of Shensi. In 1937 Japan invaded war-torn China. The survivors of the Long March became heroes of China's Communist revolution in 1949.

Mao Zedong on the Long March

In the Soviet Union, the Communist dictator Stalin ruthlessly eliminated anyone who opposed him. During his agricultural reforms, millions of people were driven from their farms and homes, many of them to die in prison camps. Soldiers, writers, musicians, artists, priests and even revolutionary politicians were among many thousands killed.

The drift towards war

The League of Nations was powerless to prevent the world sliding towards war. The western democracies ignored the danger signs. Adolf Hitler became Germany's leader in 1933. He boasted of a big new German empire, or Reich, and the Nazis began a vicious campaign against Jews. Hitler built up the German army, navy and air force. In 1938 he seized Austria and threatened Czechoslovakia. In 1939 Germany invaded Poland; Britain and France were bound by treaty to come to Poland's aid. They declared war on Germany, beginning World War II.

THE RISE OF THE DICTATORS

The First World War ended with both sides devastated by the terrible cost of the slaughter. In Europe, weak governments could not satisfy the hopes of their citizens for a better life. There was peace, but for millions of people there was no prosperity. In Japan, Italy, Germany, Spain and Portugal, democratic government sank under a tide of dictatorship. In the Soviet Union the Communist revolution was twisted into tyranny by Stalin.

The dictators wielded their power ruthlessly. They controlled the army and police, censored radio, newspapers and films, and crushed all opposition.

Italy was the first European country to fall to a dictator: Benito Mussolini, leader of a private army of blackshirted Fascists. With a promise to end strikes and disorder, Mussolini and his supporters, in 1922, marched on Rome. The King of Italy gave in and made Mussolini prime minister.

▷ Hitler reviews 'storm-troopers', members of the Nazi private army. Hitler believed Germans belonged to a 'superior race', destined to rule others. The Nazis spread their message of hate by propaganda, control of the press, radio and films, and used marches and rallies to whip up support. The Gestapo (secret police) terrorized anyone who opposed the Nazis.

DICTATORSHIP IN EUROPE

1922 Italian Fascists march on Rome. Benito Mussolini becomes prime minister.
1923 Adolf Hitler, Nazi leader, imprisoned after attempt to seize power in Bavaria, Germany.
1924 Soviet leader Lenin dies. After some plotting against rivals, Joseph Stalin becomes leader in 1928.
1932 Antonio de Salazar becomes Portugal's dictator.
1933 Hitler made Chancellor (chief minister) of Germany. Germany leaves League of Nations.
1934 Hitler becomes Führer (leader) of Germany.
1936 General Franco leads revolt of army against Spanish government. Italy and Germany back his Nationalist forces in Civil War against Republicans.
1938 Germany takes over Austria.
1939 Germany takes Czechoslovakia, then invades Poland. World War II begins.

Map legend:
- neutral
- at war
- Greatest extent of Axis (German and Italian) influence, Nov 1942.

Britain
Russia
Netherlands
Poland
Belgium
Germany
Czechoslovakia
France
Austria Hungary
Romania
Italy
Yugoslavia
Bulgaria
Spain
Albania
Greece
Turkey

△ In the 1930s the shadow of dictatorship threatened freedom in Europe. The most cruel regimes were in Nazi Germany and the Communist USSR. The dictators (see right) promised their people much, but the cost was high: no democracy, rule by fear, and persecution of 'enemies of the state'.

△ Francisco Franco (1892–1975) led a military revolt against Spain's Republican government in 1936. Victorious, he ruled Spain for 36 years.

△ Joseph Stalin 1879–1953) led the USSR from 1928 until his death. In the 1930s millions of Soviet citizens were sent to labour camps.

△ The Nazis adopted the clockwise swastika as their symbol in the 1920s. In Nazi-occupied Europe, the swastika became a hated emblem of occupation, oppression and terror.

△ Benito Mussolini (1883–1945) was once a socialist. As Italy's dictator he was backed by big business and the armed forces.

△ Adolf Hitler (1889–1945) was an evil tyrant. He murdered his opponents, exterminated Jews, and led his country into a disastrous war.

The Nazis in Germany

Germany paid heavily for its 'war guilt'. During the 1920s many Germans were without work; many lost their savings as German money became worthless.

The National Socialists (Nazis), led by Adolf Hitler, blamed foreigners for Germany's plight. They vowed to make Germany strong again and won support in elections. Once Hitler was in power, there were no more free elections in Germany, and the Nazi terror began. Germany began to rearm and to demand new territory: the world was a step nearer a second great war.

FIGHTING FOR PEACE

The war that began in 1939 in Europe soon engulfed much of the world. The Allies, including Britain, faced the Axis powers (Germany, Italy, Japan) in two main battle-grounds: Europe and North Africa, and Asia and the Pacific.

At first, German armies won startling victories in Europe (see right). France surrendered, and only Britain's air force and strong navy saved Britain from invasion.

Italy joined Germany, and the war spread to the Balkans and North Africa. Britain and the Allies were hard-pressed. Then, in the summer of 1941, Germany invaded the Soviet Union. This was Hitler's greatest mistake. After bitter fighting, his all-conquering armies came to a halt there; winter snow and dogged Russian resistance checked the German war machine.

Defeat for the Axis

The United States stayed out of the war until December 1941, when Japan attacked the US base at Pearl Harbor, Hawaii (see page 41). In its bid to control all South-East Asia, Japan sought to destroy the US fleet.

A German army attack

⊛ BLITZKRIEG IN EUROPE

In 1940 and 1941, German armies conquered most of Europe and North Africa and drove far into the Soviet Union. Tanks and motorized troops sped across country, often surrounding enemy positions, while aeroplanes bombed towns, roads and railways. This *Blitzkrieg* (German for 'lightning war') was very different from the trench warfare of the First World War. Bomber aircraft were used to raid cities, and fighter planes to attack the bombers. At sea, German submarines sank many Allied merchant ships.

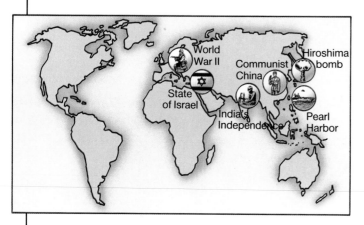

△ The Second World War was fought across Europe, North Africa, Asia and the Pacific. The war left the United States as the world's strongest power.

By 1950 most of eastern Europe and China had Communist governments. India and Pakistan were independent democracies. Israel had been founded.

1939–1945

1939 World War II begins.
1940 France defeated. Germany overruns Low Countries and Norway.
1941 Germany invades Yugoslavia, Greece, USSR. War extends to North Africa.
Japanese attack Pearl Harbor; USA enters war.
1942 Japan captures Philippines, Singapore, Dutch East Indies, Burma. Sea battles of Coral Sea, Midway (Pacific).
1943 Allies victorious in North Africa.
Italy invaded by Allies.
1944 D-Day landings in Europe. France liberated.
1945 Germany surrenders (May).
Atomic bombs dropped on two Japanese cities. Japan surrenders (August).

1945–1950

1945–8 Soviet-backed Communist governments take over in Eastern Europe.
1946 Civil war in China. Vietnamese fight against French colonial rule.
1946 Nuremberg trials of Nazi war criminals.
1947 India and Pakistan independent.
1948 Berlin airlift (Germany); Cold War threatens new world war. Reconstruction of Europe begins, with US aid (Marshall Plan).
1948 Israel founded; war between Jews and Arabs.
1949 NATO alliance founded by Western nations.
1949 Apartheid in South Africa.
1949 Communists win power in China.
1950 Start of Korean War.

Japanese planes attack Pearl Harbor

◁ The Pacific war was fought at sea as the Allies regained Japanese conquests.

Despite its early success, Japan could not match the strength of the United States. There were fierce sea battles in the Pacific, with hand-to-hand fighting on land.

The first important victory for the Allies came in the North African desert, at El Alamein in Egypt, in 1942. In 1943 the Germans began to retreat from the Soviet Union, and the Allies invaded Italy. Italy's dictator Mussolini was overthrown, and Italy surrendered. On 6 June 1944, known as D-Day, the Allies landed in France, and by 1945 Allied armies were converging on Germany.

The fighting in Europe ended in May 1945. Adolf Hitler killed himself. The advancing Allied armies uncovered the horrors of the Nazi concentration camps, where millions of Jews and others were murdered.

The Pacific war ended in August 1945, after US planes dropped atomic bombs (see below), and Japan surrendered.

⦿ THE WAR IN ASIA

Japanese planes attacked US warships at Pearl Harbor on 7 December 1941, but missed the US aircraft carriers; these ships and their planes later helped win the sea battles of the Pacific war. The war in Asia was of two halves. First, in 1941–2, Japan captured the Philippines, Malaya, Burma and the Dutch East Indies. China was near defeat, and India under threat. Then, in 1943–4, the Allies began to push back the Japanese. US forces recaptured the Pacific islands, and, by 1945, British troops had won back Burma.

⦿ HIROSHIMA: WEAPONS OF MASS DESTRUCTION

The Japanese fought fiercely; it was against their soldiers' code of honour to surrender, even when defeated. Their pilots made suicide attacks on US ships. The Allies feared huge losses on both sides if their armies invaded Japan, as they had Germany. Allied scientists had developed a

terrifying new weapon: the atomic bomb. The Allies decided to use atomic bombs to force Japan into immediate and unconditional surrender. One bomb devastated the city of Hiroshima on 6 August 1945. A second bomb destroyed Nagasaki three days later, and Japan surrendered.

Hiroshima after the A-bomb explosion (inset)

▶ THE STATE OF ISRAEL

In the 1800s Jews began settling in Palestine, the Holy Land they had once been forced to leave. Faced with anti-Semitism (victimization of Jews) in eastern Europe, Jews calling themselves Zionists determined to work for a Palestinian homeland. However, Palestine had been Arab land since the AD 600s. After the Second World War, the United Nations proposed dividing British-ruled Palestine into Arab and Jewish states. Many Jewish refugees migrated to Palestine. On 14 May 1948, Zionists declared the state of Israel. War with the Arabs broke out, and there has been no settled peace ever since.

Exodus 1947: Jewish refugees from Europe to Palestine

EUROPE

1939 Spanish Civil War ends.
1939 World War II begins. Germany and USSR agree not to fight.
1940 German victories in Denmark, Norway, Low Countries, France. Italy joins war on Germany's side.
Battle of Britain; start of blitz (air raids) on Britain.
1941 Germany invades USSR and Balkans.
1942 Battle of Stalingrad (USSR).
1943 Italy invaded by Allies, surrenders.
1944 Allies invade western Europe to free German-occupied countries. Soviets attack from east.
1944 First V2 rocket attacks on Britain.
1945 War in Europe ends. Germany surrenders.
1947 Civil war in Greece.
1948 Communists take over eastern Europe. Allies fly supplies into Berlin to break Soviet blockade.
1949 NATO alliance formed. Germany divided.

The Cold War

The Second World War was the most destructive in history. About 30 million people died, and much of Europe was in ruins, its homes and factories bombed or shelled into rubble. Many thousands of people were homeless refugees. Germany was divided, and Japan was occupied by the Allies. Among the victors, only the United States came out of the war stronger than it had been before it went in.

In 1945 the Allies founded the United Nations Organization, in an attempt to stop further wars. But the newly won peace was uneasy. Advancing on Germany, the Soviet Union had occupied much of eastern Europe, where Communist governments soon took power. East and West, no longer allies, became enemies in the new 'Cold War'.

▼ INDIA'S INDEPENDENCE

Since 1920, when M. K. Gandhi became leader of the National Congress party, India's call for independence from Britain had grown louder. After the Second World War, the British offered independence. But India's Muslims, led by M. A. Jinnah, wanted a separate country. In 1947, following bloodshed by both Muslims and Hindus, India was divided into Hindu India, led by Jawaharlal Nehru, and Muslim Pakistan, led by Jinnah. More bloodshed followed after partition.

Post-colonial India

ASIA	AFRICA	AMERICA	PACIFIC
1941 Japan attacks US Pearl Harbor (Hawaii). **1942** Japanese capture Philippines, Singapore, Dutch East Indies, Burma. Naval battles of Coral Sea and Midway, won by USA. **1944** Allies begin reconquest of the Philippines and Burma. **1945** Allies drop atomic bombs on Japanese cities. Japan surrenders (10 August). **1946** Civil war in China between Communists and Nationalists. Start of Vietnamese war against French. **1947** India and Pakistan become independent. **1948** Korea divided into North and South. **1948** Mahatma Gandhi assassinated in India. **1948** Creation of modern Israel; war between Israelis and Arabs. **1949** Indonesia wins independence from Dutch rule. **1949** Communists, led by Mao Zedong, victorious in China. **1950** Korean War begins.	**1941** Italians driven out of Somalia, Eritrea and Ethiopia. War in North Africa between German and Italian armies and Allies. **1942** Battle of El-Alamein, won by Allies. Allies land in Morocco and Algeria. **1943** Germany and Italy defeated in Africa. **1945** End of World War II: nationalist movements begin to demand independence from old colonial rule. **1947** France refuses to grant Algeria self-government. **1948** Egypt takes part in Arab war against Israel. **1949** South Africa's white government introduces apartheid (separation of the races).	**1939** USA remains neutral as World War II begins. **1941** USA leases warships to Britain. Japan attacks US base at Pearl Harbor. USA, Britain and Canada declare war on Japan. Germany and Italy declare war on USA. **1942** First nuclear pile tested in Chicago. Brazil enters war on Allies' side. **1943** US navy victorious in Pacific; tide turns against Japanese. **1944** US and Canadian forces play major part in Allied invasion of Europe. **1945** US planes drop atomic bombs on Japan. United Nations charter signed at San Francisco. Harry Truman succeeds F.D. Roosevelt as US President. **1945** President Vargas of Brazil overthrown. **1946** Juan Peron president of Argentina. **1950** Vargas returned to power in Brazil.	**1940** Australian and New Zealand forces fight in North Africa and Greece. **1941** Japanese forces sweep across the Pacific. Australia is threatened. **1942** Australian troops placed under US command in Pacific War. Naval battles of Java Sea (Japanese victory), Coral Sea, Midway (Allied victories). **1943** Japanese forced out of Guadalcanal in the Solomon Islands. **1944** Fighting ends in New Guinea. Allies win battles of the Philippine Sea (near Guam) and Leyte Gulf, involving 282 warships. **1945** US troops capture Iwo Jima, south of Japan. Victory in the Pacific. **1949** Robert Menzies becomes Australia's prime minister. Start of Snowy Mountains irrigation and hydroelectric scheme (Australia).

⏷ CHINA'S REVOLUTION

Communists, led by Mao Zedong, gained control of much of northern China during the Second World War. They began a rural revolution by giving land to the peasants. In 1946 fighting broke out again between Communists and the Nationalist government of China, led by Chiang Kai-shek (see page 37). The Communists won, and Mao became leader of the People's Republic of China in 1949. The Nationalists fled to the island of Taiwan. Mao's 'Five Year Plan' to make China an industrial power to rival the West set millions of people to work in mines, in factories and on farms.

Chinese Communists

In 1949 the United States and its allies formed the North Atlantic Treaty Organization (NATO) for defence against the Soviet Union. The Soviets responded in 1955 with a rival alliance called the Warsaw Pact.

Asian power grows

After years of struggle, India gained independence from British rule in 1947 (see page 42). The Middle East, where oil from once-poor desert states had become a vital energy source, became a new trouble spot. The state of Israel was founded, and many Jews from Europe settled there (see page 42).

China became the world's most populous Communist state after the revolution (see left). It was again isolated, as it had been in earlier times. In 1950 China challenged the United Nations in a war over Korea.

NEW WORLD, NEW HOPES

As the 1950s began, the United States was the strongest nation in the world. Under President Harry Truman, it led the so-called 'free world' in the Cold War against Communism. The Americans already had the atomic bomb, and in 1952 they tested the far more powerful hydrogen bomb. US factories had made the ships, tanks and guns with which the Allies had defeated Germany and Japan. America now helped to rebuild Europe and Japan through the economic aid package known as the Marshall Plan.

The American dream

America was still the 'promised land' of opportunity for immigrants. Most Americans enjoyed a higher standard of living than anyone else. They had better homes, more food on their tables, and a wide choice of consumer goods.

American factories had escaped being bombed in the war, and they now led the way in making new products ranging from computers to jet planes and plastics. There was plenty of work for everyone.

Justice for all Americans

Unfortunately, few black Americans shared in this prosperity. In the 1950s, black leaders began to protest against unfair treatment, including racial segregation (separation of blacks and whites) in schools in the Southern states. This was the start of the modern American Civil Rights movement.

▽ Cookery class in a US girls' school. Many American girls still looked forward to marriage and motherhood, but some, were seeking careers in business and politics.

USA IN THE 1950s

1950 Senator McCarthy leads inquiry into 'un-American activities'.
1951 Colour television broadcasts by CBS.
1952 Dwight D. Eisenhower ('Ike') becomes President.
1952 USA tests first hydrogen bomb.
1954 Supreme Court rules against segregation of blacks and whites in schools.
1957 Civil Rights Act passed: race riots in South.
1958 Videotape invented. First US jet airliner, Boeing 707, in service.
1958 First US space satellite.
1959 US engineers develop the microchip.

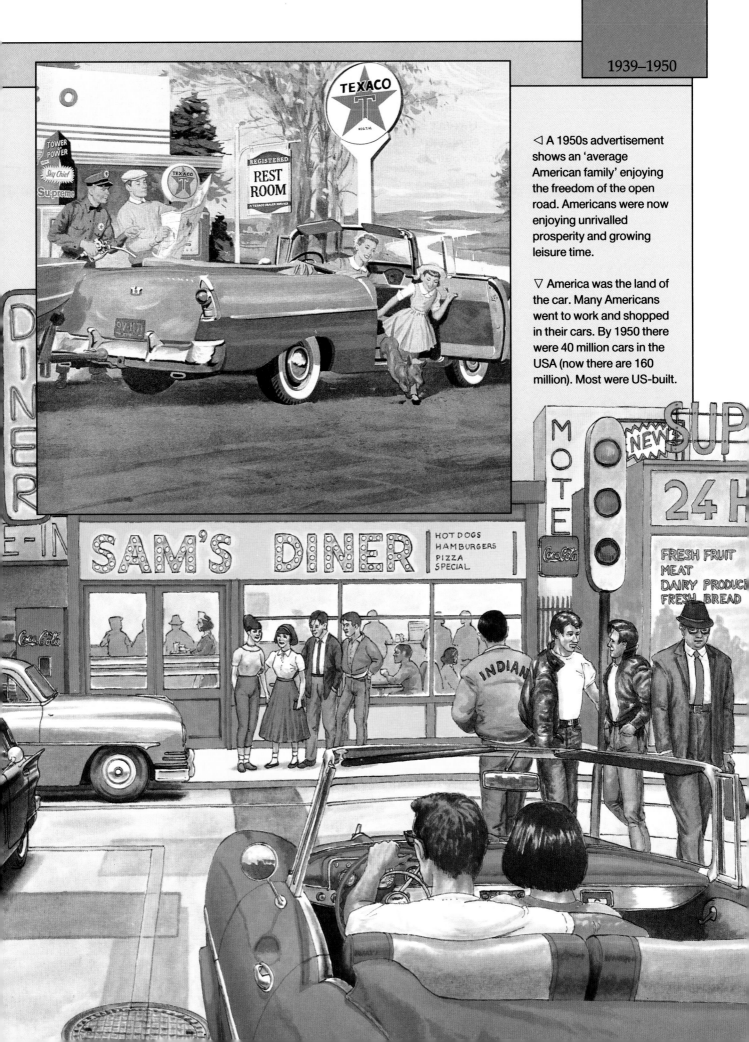

◁ A 1950s advertisement shows an 'average American family' enjoying the freedom of the open road. Americans were now enjoying unrivalled prosperity and growing leisure time.

▽ America was the land of the car. Many Americans went to work and shopped in their cars. By 1950 there were 40 million cars in the USA (now there are 160 million). Most were US-built.

DISUNITED NATIONS

During the 1950s the United States and the Soviet Union – the world's superpowers – each built up massive arsenals of nuclear bombs and rockets. In the atmosphere of Cold War, neither trusted the other and there were several flashpoints (see page 47).

Change in Europe

Europe slowly rebuilt after the Second World War. In 1957 six nations – France, West Germany, Italy, Belgium, the Netherlands and Luxembourg – form the European Economic Community or Common Market.

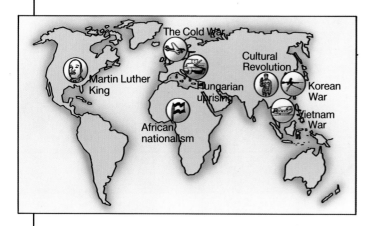

West Germany prospered and, by the 1960s, was the strongest industrial country in Europe. Communist East Germany lagged behind. In 1961 its government built the Berlin Wall to stop East Germans fleeing to the West via West Berlin.

West Germany and France, former enemies, became partners. France's President from 1958 to 1969 was the wartime resistance leader, General Charles De Gaulle.

Old empires and new nations

By 1954 France had left Vietnam and its other Indo-Chinese colonies. Vietnam was torn by a civil war in which the United States became deeply involved by the 1960s (see page 48). In 1956, when Egypt nationalized the Suez Canal, Britain and France tried to use force to regain control of it, but failed.

▼ AFRICAN NATIONALISM

In the 1950s and 1960s, black leaders such as Kenya's Jomo Kenyatta and Ghana's Kwame Nkrumah took power in Africa's new nations. The first black African colony to gain its freedom was Ghana (formerly the Gold Coast) in 1957. Europeans had drawn the map of colonial Africa, and often the new nations' boundaries ignored tribal and regional loyalties. This sometimes caused difficulties. Some of Africa's new nations were very poor, with few resources. Many, such as the former Belgian Congo (now Zaire), suffered from civil wars after independence.

△ African colonies became independent. The European Economic Community was founded. The USA and USSR were rivals. Vietnam and the Middle East were trouble-spots. Japan became a trade force.

▷ Africa had new flags and new leaders, as former colonies became independent.

1950–1960
1953 End of Korean War. **1953** Death of Soviet dictator Stalin. **1956** Britain and France attack Egypt over Suez Canal. Second Arab–Israeli war. **1956** Uprising in Hungary. **1957** First space satellite, *Sputnik 1* (USSR). **1957** Ghana (Gold Coast) independent. **1957** European Economic Community (EEC) founded. **1959** Communist revolution in Cuba. **1960** John F. Kennedy elected new US President. **1960** Former colonies in Africa independent.

1960–1970
1961 East Germans build Berlin Wall. Yuri Gagarin (USSR), first astronaut. **1962** Cuba missile crisis: USA and USSR draw back from war. **1963** President Kennedy assassinated. USA in Vietnam War. **1965** Rhodesia declares illegal independence. **1966** Cultural Revolution in China. **1967** Third Arab–Israeli war. **1968** Soviet invasion of Czechoslovakia. **1969** US astronauts land on the Moon.

△ Soviet tanks in the streets of Budapest during Hungary's 1956 uprising against Soviet domination.

▽ Allied planes flew supplies into West Berlin when it was blockaded by the USSR in 1948–9.

▼ COLD WAR

The Cold War was a power struggle between, on the one side, the Soviet Union and its Communist allies (the Eastern bloc) and, on the other the United States and its allies (the 'free' West). It started in 1945 when the Soviet Union, suspicious of the West, took over much of eastern Europe and began to set up Communist governments there. Incidents such as the Berlin airlift (1948) and the Hungarian uprising (1956) came close to starting a real war. Communist China confronted the West during the Korean War (1950–3). The Cold War was at its height in the 1950s and early 1960s. In the 1970s, both East and West realized that neither side could win a nuclear war, and disarmament agreements marked the beginning of the end of the Cold War.

EAST–WEST CONFLICT

1945 End of Second World War.
1945–8 Communist take-over in eastern Europe.
1948 Berlin airlift. Korea divided.
1949 Germany divided into West and East (Communist). North Atlantic Treaty Organization founded.
1950–3 Korean War.
1956 Hungarian uprising.
1961 Berlin Wall built.
1962 Cuban missile crisis.
1968 Soviets halt democracy movement in Czechoslovakia.

Independence in Africa

Most European-ruled African colonies gained independence (see page 46). In West Africa, this came about peacefully. In North Africa, the French left Algeria, where there were many French settlers, in 1962, but only after a war. In East Africa, most former British colonies were independent by the end of the 1960s. But some white settlers resisted change. Rhodesia's whites declared an illegal independence in 1965, refusing to share power with blacks, and war resulted. Africa's richest country, white-ruled South Africa, became a republic in 1961. Its policy of racial separation (apartheid) made it an outcast among the world's nations. Of Europe's old colonial powers, only Portugal held on to its African colonies into the 1970s.

▽ The Korean War was a test of strength between the UN (defending South Korea) and Communist North Korea and China.

The war lasted over three years. Neither side won, and Korea has remained divided between North and South.

US troops in Vietnam

The Soviet Empire

Stalin ruled the Soviet Union until his death in 1953. Under his successors Nikita Khrushchev and Leonid Brezhnev, industry was modernized and Soviet space triumphs astonished the world (see pages 50-51). But Soviet farms rarely produced enough food for the people, who had few luxuries.

Fearful of change, the Soviet government sent the Red Army to crush opposition in Hungary (1956) and Czechoslovakia (1968).

The Cuba crisis

In 1959, Communists seized power on Cuba, a Caribbean island. The Cuban leader, Fidel Castro, sought aid from the Soviet Union. In 1962, US spy planes spotted Soviet missiles on the island aimed at America. A war between the superpowers seemed possible, until Khrushchev removed the weapons.

ⓐ WAR IN VIETNAM

The French left Vietnam in 1954, with the country split between the Communist North and the non-Communist South. When elections to unify the country were called off, Vietcong (Communist) guerrillas attacked the South. The USA sent troops to aid the South and by 1969, 540,000 Americans were fighting in Vietnam. But despite intense bombing of the North, the US failed to win the war. In 1973 the last US soldier left Vietnam, and two years later the country was unified under the Communists.

EUROPE	ASIA	AFRICA	AMERICA
1952 Queen Elizabeth II becomes head of Commonwealth. **1953** Tito is President of Communist Yugoslavia. **1955** Communist states form Warsaw Pact alliance. **1956** Soviet army puts down Hungarian uprising. **1957** Treaty of Rome sets up EEC. Founder members are Belgium, France, Italy, Luxembourg, Netherlands, West Germany. **1958** Charles De Gaulle is President of France's Fifth Republic. **1961** Berlin Wall built by East Germans. **1962** First live television satellite link between USA and Europe. **1964** Civil War in Cyprus. **1964** Soviet leader Nikita Khrushchev succeeded by Leonid Brezhnev. **1967** Army take over government of Greece. **1968** Soviet army invades Czechoslovakia. **1969** Britain sends troops to Northern Ireland.	**1950–3** Korean War ended by Treaty of Panmunjon. **1951** China invades Tibet. Colombo Plan, for economic development in South and South-East Asia. **1953** Mount Everest climbed for first time. **1954** Viet Minh defeat French in Vietnam, which is divided into North and South. South-East Asia Treaty Organization (SEATO) formed. **1956** Arab–Israeli war. **1959** Revolt in Tibet put down by Chinese. Dalai Lama, Tibetan leader, exiled in India. **1964** War between Indonesia and Malaysia. **1965** India and Pakistan at war. **1965** US troops fighting in Vietnam. Singapore independent. **1966** Cultural Revolution in China. **1967** Six-Day War between Arabs and Israelis. Israel captures West Bank of Jordan river, and Jerusalem. **1968** North Vietnamese attack South Vietnam.	**1952** Unrest in Kenya: Mau Mau terrorists. **1953** Egypt a republic. **1956** Egypt nationalizes Suez Canal. Britain and France invade, but soon withdraw. **1960** Seventeen African colonies become independent. **1960** Civil war in Congo: Katanga province breaks away. **1961** South Africa becomes a republic and leaves the Commonwealth. **1962** Algeria independent from France after eight years of war. **1963–5** Kenya, Malawi, Zambia, Gambia, Tanzania, Botswana, Lesotho become independent. **1965** British colony of Rhodesia declares independence with a whites-only government. **1966** South African premier Dr Verwoerd assassinated. **1967** Civil war in Nigeria; eastern region (Biafra) breaks away. **1970** End of Nigerian war; Biafra defeated.	**1950** Anti-Communist campaign in USA. **1952** Dwight Eisenhower US President. **1955** Argentina's President Peron exiled. **1957** US Civil Rights Act passed. **1959** Communist revolution in Cuba, led by Fidel Castro. **1959** St Lawrence Seaway opened in Canada. **1960** John F. Kennedy US President. **1960** Invasion of Cuba by anti-Communists fails. **1962** Cuban missile crisis. **1962** Jamaica, Trinidad and Tobago independent. **1963** President Kennedy assassinated. Lyndon B. Johnson succeeds him. **1968** Martin Luther King, US black civil rights leader, and Robert Kennedy, brother of President Kennedy, assassinated. **1968** Richard Nixon elected US President. **1968–79** Pierre Trudeau Canadian prime minister. **1969** US *Apollo 11* spacecraft lands first astronauts on the Moon.

China and Japan

China experienced massive changes under its Communist government. In 1966 the Chinese leader Mao Zedong set the country in turmoil when he tried to reshape Chinese society by 'Cultural Revolution' (see below).

Japan prospered. New Japanese factories turned out cars, motorcycles and electrical goods that were sold all over the world.

Middle East wars

The Middle East supplied the industrial world with much of the oil that it needed. Some Middle Eastern countries, such as Saudi Arabia, were rich. Others were poorer and were troubled by wars and revolutions.

Israel fought victorious wars against its Arab neighbours in 1956 and 1967. Some Arab nationalists wanted to regain Palestine and unite all the Arab peoples under Islam.

North and South America

Economic progress in South America was held back by corrupt governments and unstable rule, with army leaders often seeking power. In the Caribbean region, Jamaica and other island states became self-governing.

John F. Kennedy became the youngest-ever President of the United States in 1960 and set the target for the Apollo programme to land Americans on the Moon before 1970 (see pages 50-51).

Kennedy's presidency ended in tragedy in 1963, when he was murdered. In 1968 his brother Robert, a candidate for President, and the black Civil Rights leader Martin Luther King were also shot dead. It was a time of unrest and unhappiness in America. Young people protested against the Vietnam War, a war that the United States, for all its power, could not win (see pages 48, 49).

PACIFIC

1951 ANZUS defence treaty signed by Australia, New Zealand and USA.
1958 First land crossing of Antarctica by Commonwealth expedition.
1960 Antarctic Treaty signed, to protect Antarctica for scientific research.
1962 Western Samoa becomes independent.
1965 Australian troops fight in Vietnam War.
1967 Suharto succeeds Sukarno as president of Indonesia.
1970 Fiji and Tonga become independent.

▼ RED CHINA

In 1966 Mao Zedong started China's 'Cultural Revolution'. Teachers and scientists were forced to work in the fields or were imprisoned. Schools were closed. Committees took over factories, and youthful 'Red Guards' marched in the streets. The chaos damaged China's economy and cost many lives.

Chinese Red Guards

▼ PROTESTS IN THE SIXTIES

Protest marches were common in the West during the 1960s. Often the protesters were students, shouting their opposition to the Vietnam War or to nuclear weapons. Some called for revolution, but most just felt that the world needed fresh ideas, to make a new start. In the United States many people demonstrated against the Vietnam War. Many thousands – black and white – also marched in support of the Civil Rights movement, demanding an end to unfair treatment of black Americans.

Martin Luther King, Civil Rights leader

THE SPACE AGE

The space age began in 1957, when the Soviet Union launched the first satellite, *Sputnik 1*. From rocket experiments in the 1920s, engineers had developed the V2 missile, used by Germany during the Second World War. After the war, the Soviet Union and the United States used German plans and scientists to help set up their own guided missile and space programmes.

First steps in space

The Soviets led the way into space because their rockets were bigger. They launched *Sputnik 2*, carrying a dog (1957), and then crashed a rocket on the Moon (1959). In 1961, Soviet cosmonaut Yuri Gagarin became the first person to orbit the Earth in space.

Americans on the Moon

The Americans were determined to be first to land on the Moon. They spent millions of dollars on the huge *Saturn 5* rocket and the three-man *Apollo* spacecraft. In the 1960s, US astronauts made regular flights in Earth orbit. In 1968, *Apollo 8* flew round the Moon and back to Earth. The following year, *Apollo 11* landed two men on the Moon.

But whereas every US lift-off and splashdown (landing at sea) was watched by millions on television, the Soviet programme was more secretive.

Artificial satellites have improved television broadcasting, weather forecasting and navigation at sea, and have also aided military reconnaissance.

▷ *Apollo 15* set down US astronauts Scott and Irwin on the Moon on 26 July 1971. The explorers drove a Lunar Rover (far right) across the Moon's surface.

THE SPACE RACE

1957 First satellite *Sputnik 1* (USSR).
1959 First weather satellite (USA).
1959 First probe hits the Moon (*Luna 2*, USSR).
1961 First person in space, Yuri Gagarin (USSR).
1962 First TV relay by satellite across Atlantic (*Telstar 1*).
1969 US astronauts land on Moon (*Apollo 11*).
1971 First soft landing on Mars (*Mars 3*, USSR).
1972 *Apollo 17* (USA), last landing on the Moon.
1976 US *Viking* probes land on Mars.
1981 First US Shuttle flight.
1983 *Pioneer 10* (USA), first space probe to travel beyond all the planets.
1986 US *Challenger* Shuttle disaster; crew killed in fire.
1988 Two Soviet astronauts spend 366 days in space station.

▽ The Soviet Union claimed a number of space firsts in the 1960s. Valentina Tereshkova was the first woman in space (in 1963). Tereshkova, a textile technologist and parachutist, had only a year's cosmonaut training.

△ In the 1950s, computers were big and slow. The Space Age brought smaller but much faster-working computers, using new microchip technology.

▽ Space rivals turned partners in 1975, when Soviet and US crews docked their *Soyuz* and *Apollo* craft for a 5-day joint mission.

51

A CHANGING WORLD

In the 1970s the Cold War power struggle between the United States and the Soviet Union reached a new stage. Both sides already had enough nuclear weapons to blow the world to ashes. The hope was that this 'nuclear deterrent' would make neither want to risk a war. Spy satellites made it easier for each to see how many weapons the other had. At last, talks on arms cuts began to make some progress.

Rich and poor worlds

In the early 1970s a worldwide energy crisis arose when Arab states cut oil production after a third Arab–Israeli war (see page 53). The price of oil rose so steeply that economies in every continent went into decline. More people began to think seriously about alternative energy sources, such as nuclear, solar (sun) and tidal power.

The European Community (EC), with 12 member countries by the 1980s, became a trading area bigger than the United States. Both the EC and USA strove to compete with Japan. Australia and New Zealand forged closer links with their Pacific neighbours.

▽ By the 1990s the USA was the only claimant to 'superpower' status. The USSR had collapsed, and the map of Europe was changing as new states emerged. Asia and South America were growing stronger. Africa was hit by famine and civil wars. Environmental problems affected the whole world.

⊙ CENTRAL AMERICA

In the 1980s there were civil wars in the Central American republics of El Salvador and Nicaragua. Both countries had earlier suffered under dictatorships, and most of their people were poor farmers. The United States became involved in both wars, with aid and military advisers. In El Salvador, the USA backed the government against socialist rebels. In Nicaragua (below), the US supported rebel *contras* against the socialist Sandinista government, until the Sandinistas were voted out of power in 1990. In 1989 US troops invaded Panama to arrest its corrupt ruler, Noriega.

Soldiers in Nicaragua

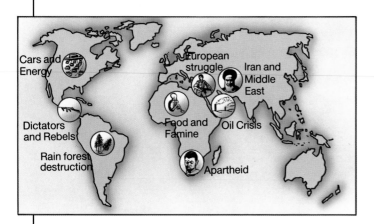

Cars and Energy

European struggle

Iran and Middle East

Dictators and Rebels

Food and Famine

Oil Crisis

Rain forest destruction

Apartheid

1970–1980

1972 Civil war in El Salvador and Lebanon.
1973 Britain, Ireland, Denmark join European Economic Community.
1973 Worldwide energy crisis after fourth Arab–Israeli war.
1974 Watergate scandal (involving bugging political opponents' HQ) in USA. President Nixon is implicated and resigns.
1975 End of Vietnam War.
1976 Death of China's leader Mao Zedong.
1978 John Paul II (Polish) first non-Italian Pope since 1500s.
1979 Islamic revolution in Iran.
1980 Soviet troops invade Afghanistan. Solidarity Union in Poland challenges Communist government.

1980 – 1990s

1980–8 War between Iran and Iraq.
1981 Greece joins European Community.
1982 Britain and Argentina at war over Falkland Islands.
1985 New era of reform in USSR under Mikhail Gorbachev.
1986 Spain and Portugal join EC.
1989 Berlin Wall opened. Collapse of Communism in Eastern Europe.
1989 Chinese government cracks down on demonstrators calling for democracy.
1990 Germany becomes one country again, after 45 years.
1990 South Africa moves towards change.
1990 Gulf War.
1991 Break-up of the USSR.

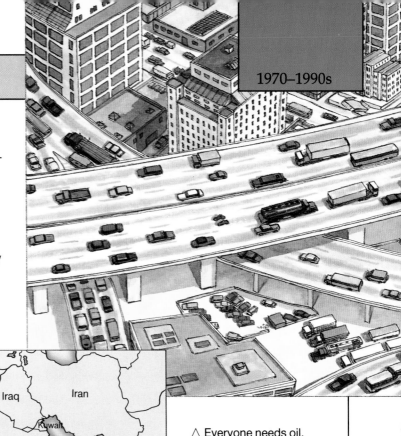

▼ THE POLITICS OF OIL

Oil is the most valuable fuel; without it, lights in cities would go out, factories fall silent, cars and trucks come to a stop. Much of the world's oil comes from the Middle East, where some countries have become immensely rich from selling the oil beneath their desert sands. Any war in the Middle East alarms the United States, Europe and Japan, which buy oil from there. In recent history, the Middle East has seen many wars: between the Arabs and Israel (1948–9, 1956, 1967, 1973), between Iran and Iraq (1980–8), and between Iraq and UN forces led by the United States (1990–1).

▷ The Middle East has about 10% of the world's oil, with Saudi Arabia the largest oil producer. The Gulf is a key waterway. Israel and its Arab neighbours have still to solve their dispute and end the Palestine problem.

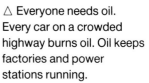

△ Everyone needs oil. Every car on a crowded highway burns oil. Oil keeps factories and power stations running.

The Yom Kippur War 1973

The Iranian revolution

The nations of the North were rich, but the countries of the South (in particular, Africa south of the Equator) were poor. Many were in debt. They had little food and too many mouths to feed (see page 55).

Religious revolution

A powerful force in world affairs was a 'fundamentalist' religious movement in Islam. In 1979 the Shah (emperor) of Iran (formerly Persia) was deposed by an Islamic revolution. Its leader, Ayatollah Khomeini, rejected Western modernization and called for a return to traditional Muslim ways. His views found support elsewhere in the Middle East, in North Africa and in Pakistan. In India, there was religious strife, involving Hindus, Muslims and Sikhs.

The Cold War ends

Since 1970 there have been numerous regional wars: in Central America (see page 52), in Africa, in the Falklands and in the Middle East.

Yet, by the 1990s, there was hope of a better world. Protecting the environment became a world concern (see page 55). South Africa seemed to be moving towards a new era (see page 55). Communism in the Soviet Union and Eastern Europe collapsed, ending the Cold War (see pages 56-57).

Towards a new century

Yet while advances in technology – in computers, telecommunications, medicine and genetics – offer hope of a brighter future, famine and disease still haunt the world.

How does the world look in the 1990s? The United Nations is far from being an effective world government. The United States is the only military superpower, and Japan the world's trade leader. South America hopes for a new era of democracy. The former Soviet republics have self-government, but there is much local unrest.

The gap between rich and poor nations is widening. Much of Africa is ravaged by civil war, disease, hunger and poverty. The Middle East remains a trouble spot, despite peace efforts. China, with more than a billion people, is still governed by Communists who are set against change.

Few historians predicted the dramatic changes of recent years. Few would forecast what will happen in the next century.

EUROPE	ASIA	AFRICA	AMERICA
1973 Britain, Ireland and Denmark join EEC. **1974** Democratic revolution in Portugal. **1974** Cyprus divided into self-governing Greek and Turkish areas. **1975** Death of Spain's dictator, Franco. Spain returns to democracy (1977) and monarchy. **1979** Margaret Thatcher becomes Britain's first woman prime minister. **1981** François Mitterrand President of France. Greece joins EC. **1982** Death of Soviet leader Leonid Brezhnev. **1985** Mikhail Gorbachev new Soviet leader starts reform programme. **1986** Chernobyl nuclear accident in USSR. **1989** Fall of Communist governments in Eastern Europe. **1990** Germany reunited. **1990s** Boris Yeltsin, Russian president. **1990s** Yugoslavia torn apart by civil war. **1991** Attempt to overthrow Gorbachev in USSR fails. Gorbachev resigns, USSR breaks up. **1993** Czechoslovakia becomes two states.	**1972** Ceylon becomes the republic of Sri Lanka. **1973** Yom Kippur War (Arab–Israeli); oil supplies cut, world energy crisis. **1975** Vietnam War ends in victory for North. Khmer Rouge seize power in Cambodia; millions die under Pol Pot's rule. **1975** Civil war in Lebanon. **1976** Mao Zedong, Chinese leader, dies. **1977** Army take-over in Pakistan. **1979** Revolution in Iraq; Islamic fundamentalists take power. **1979** War between China and Vietnam. **1979** Afghanistan invaded by Soviet troops. **1980–8** Iran–Iraq war. **1984** India's prime minister Indira Gandhi assassinated. **1989** Chinese government crushes pro-democracy movement. **1990–1** Gulf War, after Iraq invades Kuwait. **1991** Rajiv Gandhi, Indian prime minister, assassinated. **1991** Middle East peace talks begin.	**1974** Portugal's African colonies (Guinea-Bissau, Angola, Mozambique) independent. Communists overthrow Emperor Haile Selassie of Ethiopia. **1976** Morocco and Mauritania divide Spanish Sahara: a nationalist revolt follows. **1979** Tanzania invades Uganda, removes dictator Idi Amin. **1980** Black majority government in Zimbabwe (formerly Rhodesia). **1981** President Sadat of Egypt assassinated. **1984** War and famine in Ethiopia. **1986** USA bombs Libya, accusing the Libyan leader Qaddafi of terrorism. **1990** Under President De Klerk, Black leader Nelson Mandela is released. Namibia independent. **1991** Ethiopia's Communist government overthrown. Zambia votes President Kaunda (ruler since 1964) out of office. South Africa abolishes apartheid. Famine and war in Sudan, Somalia and Mozambique.	**1973** Chile's President Allende overthrown. **1974** US President Nixon resigns: Gerald Ford takes over. **1977** Jimmy Carter becomes US President. **1979** Panama Canal Zone transferred from USA to Panama. Nicaragua's dictator Somoza deposed. **1981** Ronald Reagan becomes US President. **1982** Argentina invades Falkland Islands. Britain recaptures islands after war. **1983** US and Caribbean troops invade Grenada. **1985** Democratic revolutions in Brazil and Uruguay. **1989** George Bush becomes US President. US invades Panama to oust dictator Noriega. **1990** Chile and Brazil return to democracy after military rule. **1991** Peace in El Salvador after civil war. **1990s** End of Sandinista rule in Nicaragua. Bill Clinton becomes US President (1993). Canada faces crisis over Quebec's status. Brazil strongest South American nation.

⊙ CHANGE IN SOUTH AFRICA

From 1950 all South Africans were classified by race. There were separate schools for whites. Only whites were allowed to vote. Black opponents of this system, called *apartheid*, faced imprisonment or exile. Change began in 1989 under a new white President, F.W. de Klerk. Black leaders Nelson Mandela (above, with his wife) and Walter Sisulu were freed from prison. Apartheid was abolished and, despite an upsurge in violence, a majority black government with Nelson Mandela as President took office in May 1994.

⊙ SAVING THE PLANET

Much of the modern world is crowded and dirty. There are nearly 6 billion people on Earth, and every year they consume more of the world's resources. The rain forests of the tropics are cut down for timber or to make way for roads and cattle ranches. Gases from cars, power stations and factories pollute the air. Waste and chemicals pollute water and soil. Wild plants and wild animals lose their natural habitats. All over the world, people have begun to see how precious the Earth's natural resources are. Governments are starting to act. At the Earth Summit meeting in Brazil in 1992, the nations addressed the problem of seeking solutions to the environmental problems facing us all.

The Gulf War

▷ Burning oil wells after the 1991 Gulf War polluted air and sea. Rain-forest destruction (below) kills a natural resource whose variety is priceless.

PACIFIC

1972 President Marcos imposes army rule in Philippines.
1975 Papua New Guinea independent.
1976 Indonesia takes over Portuguese East Timor.
1979 Kiribati (Gilbert Islands) independent.
1980 Vanuatu (New Hebrides) independent.
1983 Brunei independent.
1986 Philippines President Marcos beaten in elections by Corazon Aquino.
1987 Army take-over in Fiji, against majority Indian population.
1991 Federated States of Micronesia and Marshall Islands independent. Paul Keating succeeds Bob Hawke as Australian prime minister.

⊙ WORLD HUNGER

Many people in Africa, Asia and Latin America die from hunger and from disease caused by poor diet. In the 1980s severe drought in parts of Africa made crops fail. Farm animals died. Families were forced to leave their homes. These terrible famines were made worse by hardship caused by civil wars. Despite relief aid, millions of people died.

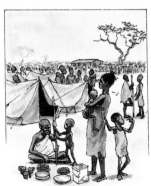

Famine victims in Africa

A NEW WORLD ORDER

In 1984 a new Soviet leader, Mikhail Gorbachev, offered an end to the Cold War. US President Ronald Reagan, who, in 1981, began his presidency by announcing a space defence system against Soviet attack, was soon shaking hands with Gorbachev and discussing disarmament. The peace process continued under Reagan's successor, President George Bush.

Gorbachev knew that the Soviet Union's military might hid the fact that its economy was weak and that its factories were old-fashioned. He wanted reform, based on openness and reconstruction. No longer would the USSR dictate to its Communist allies in Eastern Europe.

The collapse of Communism in Europe

In 1989 the break-up of the Communist bloc began. Across Eastern Europe, in Poland, Romania, Czechoslovakia, Hungary, Bulgaria – and even isolated Albania – revolutions deposed the old leaders and moved these countries towards a more Western-style government and economy.

East Germany, the most unyielding of Communist states, tottered. No longer penned in by border guards and barbed wire, hundreds of East Berliners drove across into West Berlin. The East German government fell. The hated Berlin Wall was demolished, and in 1990 Germany was united for the first time since 1945.

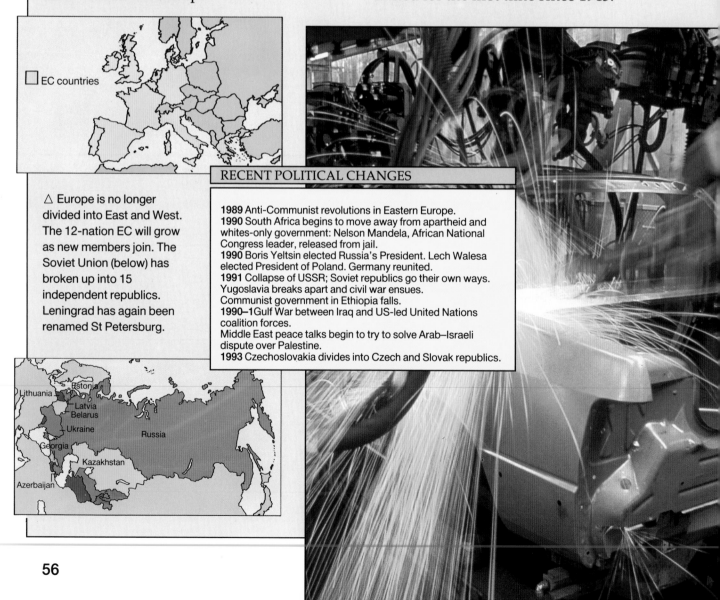

☐ EC countries

△ Europe is no longer divided into East and West. The 12-nation EC will grow as new members join. The Soviet Union (below) has broken up into 15 independent republics. Leningrad has again been renamed St Petersburg.

RECENT POLITICAL CHANGES

1989 Anti-Communist revolutions in Eastern Europe.
1990 South Africa begins to move away from apartheid and whites-only government: Nelson Mandela, African National Congress leader, released from jail.
1990 Boris Yeltsin elected Russia's President. Lech Walesa elected President of Poland. Germany reunited.
1991 Collapse of USSR; Soviet republics go their own ways. Yugoslavia breaks apart and civil war ensues. Communist government in Ethiopia falls.
1990–1 Gulf War between Iraq and US-led United Nations coalition forces.
Middle East peace talks begin to try to solve Arab–Israeli dispute over Palestine.
1993 Czechoslovakia divides into Czech and Slovak republics.

Lithuania
Estonia
Latvia
Belarus
Ukraine
Georgia
Russia
Kazakhstan
Azerbaijan

The end of the Soviet Union

Soviet leader Gorbachev was popular abroad, but at home his people demanded more goods in the shops. There was unrest and fighting in several Soviet republics. In 1991 Gorbachev was almost deposed by Communist diehards, who feared that change would bring about chaos. The Soviet Union was breaking up, into 15 separate republics, and Gorbachev resigned; he had nothing left to rule. Boris Yeltsin, leader of the largest new republic, Russia, began his own programme to reform the economy.

Freedom brought rejoicing, but also fears for the future, and danger as old rivalries resurfaced. The break-up of Communist Yugoslavia led to savage fighting among Serbs, Bosnian Muslims and Croats. Parts of Africa were also torn by civil war. The world map may change, but the old problems remain.

△ Germans clamber onto the Berlin Wall, no longer afraid of being shot by East German guards. By 1990, after almost 30 years, the Wall was gone.

◁ In the industrial world, robots can now take over repetitive jobs from human workers. Old industries give way to new, old skills to new ones, sometimes changing the fabric of society itself.

▷ An aid worker from a developed country – part of the First World – provides medical help to people in Burkino Faso, west Africa – a developing, or Third World, country – to raise its standard of living.

TIMECHART 1

REVOLUTIONS

The Modern World has been shaped by revolutions in government, social life, science and technology. These changes began to affect people in many countries in the 1800s, and continued at an even faster rate in the 1900s.

Political
The French revolutionaries of 1789 wanted reform: a new government, new laws, equality for all. They wanted a fresh beginning, though few had a clear idea of what kind of society they would like to see created. The French Revolution inspired other freedom movements in other countries. During the 1800s reformers fought for justice and social change. They demanded an end to slavery and children working in factories. They founded trade unions to improve workers' conditions, and campaigned for improvements in public health.

Arts and Science
The writers and artists who belonged to the Romantic movement early in the 1800s believed, above all, in individual freedom. They feared that in the new industrial age of machines, people would lose touch with the truth and beauty of Nature. Science taught that only what could be proved was real. Darwin's theories of evolution suggested that humans, like all living things, had evolved from earlier forms. So was the account of the Creation in the Bible just a story? The argument still goes on today.

Industrial
Science and industry together altered the world. Steam trains and steam ships were common by the 1850s. In the 1880s came cars, in the early 1900s aeroplanes. Gas and electric light replaced candles. Inventions such as the mechanical reaper, camera, telephone and typewriter changed daily life. There were life-saving advances in medicine, such as anaesthetics and antiseptic surgery. Science also made new weapons that killed more efficiently. Napoleon's battles were bloody, but many more soldiers died in the gunfire of the American Civil War and the Franco–Prussian War. The horrors of two World Wars were still to come.

EUROPE

1789 French Revolution begins.
1792 France at war with Austria and Prussia
1792 Gas lighting invented.
1793 Execution of Louis XVI, King of France.
1799 Consulate in France.
1800 First electric battery.
1804 Napoleon Emperor of France.
1804 First steam locomotive.
1807 Britain abolishes slavery in its Empire.
1808–14 Peninsular War.
1812 Napoleon invades Russia.
1814 Napoleon exiled to Elba.
1815 Battle of Waterloo. Congress of Vienna. End of Napoleonic Wars
1821 Greek independence.
1821 Faraday invents dynamo.
1825 First passenger-carrying steam railway.
1830 Louis Philippe "citizen-king" of France.
1837 Victoria Queen of Britain.
1838 First electric telegraph.
1846 Famine in Ireland.
1848 Year of Revolutions.
1852 Second Empire in France: Napoleon III.
1854–6 Crimean War.
1859 Darwin's *The Origin of Species* published.
1860–61 Italy united, except Venice and Rome.
1861 Pasteur shows that germs cause disease.
1866 Prussia defeats Austria.
1870 Italian unity complete.
1870 Franco–Prussian War. France defeated.
1871 German Empire.
1871 Paris Commune.
1885 First motor car, in Germany.

First petrol-powered car 1885

ASIA

1793 Unsuccessful British diplomatic mission to China.
1794 Qaja dynasty in Persia.
1796 Britain conquers Ceylon (Sri Lanka), from Dutch.
1818 British defeat Marathas in India.
1819 Raffles founds British colony of Singapore.
1824 First British–Burmese War.
1825 Dutch defeat Javanese.
1830 Russia begins conquest of Kazakhstan.
1839 Opium War between China and Britain.
1842 China hands over Hong Kong to Britain.
1845 War between British and Sikhs in India.
1850 Taiping rebellion, China.
1854 USA forces Japan to open its ports to Western trade.
1856–60 Britain and China at war again.
1857 Indian Mutiny; British crush uprising.
1860 British and French occupy Beijing.
1863 Start of French empire in Indo–China.
1867 End of Shogun rule in Japan, start of Meiji modernization period.
1877 Queen Victoria proclaimed Empress of India.

Queen Victoria of Great Britain made Empress of India 1877

1885 Indian National Congress meets for first time.
1891 Russians start building Trans-Siberian Railway.
1894 Japan and China at war.
1895 Japan defeats China in war, gains Formosa (Taiwan). Korea Japanese-controlled.
1900 Boxer Rebellion in China against foreigners.

AFRICA

1795 British take Cape of Good Hope from Dutch.
1798 French invade Egypt.
1810 Chaka organizes Zulu armies, goes on to found empire.
1830 France colonizes Algeria.
1835 Boers begin Great Trek.
1851 British capture Lagos in Nigeria.
1852 David Livingstone (Britain) begins first journey into central Africa.
1862 John Hanning Speke (Britain) discovers source of River Nile.
1869 Suez Canal is opened.
1871 Henry Morton Stanley (USA) and Livingstone meet on shore of Lake Tanganyika.

Stanley meets Livingstone 1871

1877 Stanley reaches Atlantic coast after exploring Congo River.
1879–80 Wars in southern Africa between British and Boers and Zulus.
1883 Boer leader Paul Kruger becomes President of Transvaal.
1884 Berlin Conference, European nations scramble to seize colonies in Africa.
1885 War in Sudan between Mahdi's forces and British–Egyptian armies.
1889 Italy claims Ethiopia.
1890 Cecil Rhodes founds Rhodesia.
1899 Start of British–Boer War in South Africa.

AMERICA

1789 George Washington first US President.
1791 Canada Act: Britain divides Canada.
1791 Toussaint l'Ouverture leads slave revolt in Haiti.
1803 USA gains Louisiana territory.
1810 Argentina independent from Spain.
1811–12 Venezuela, Paraguay and Colombia independent.
1812–15 War between Britain and USA.
1820s Liberation struggles in South America.
1822 Brazil independent.
1828 Uruguay independent.
1836 Texas wins independence from Mexico.
1840 Act of Union joins Upper and Lower Canada.

Wagon trains head west 1840s

1840s Wagon trains of settlers move westward into new US territories.
1845 US–Mexican War.
1848 California gold rush (USA).
1861–5 American Civil War between Northern and Southern states.
1863 President Lincoln frees black slaves of the USA.
1867 USA buys Alaska from Russia.
1869 First railway across the USA.
1876 Battle of Little Bighorn, Indians defeat US army.
1885 First railway across Canada.
1898 Spanish–American War.

PACIFIC

1791 Sealers, whalers and missionaries visit New Zealand.
1801–3 Flinders (Britain) sails around Australia.
1803 Van Diemen's Land (now Tasmania) becomes penal colony.
1808 The Rum Rebellion in New South Wales.
1825 Revolt in Java put down by Dutch.
1828 Western Australia founded.
1834 South Australia founded.
1840 New Zealand becomes a British colony.
1845 Maori rebellion in New Zealand.
1850 Australian colonies granted self-government.

Gold panning in Australia 1850s

1851 Gold rush in Australia.
1860 Second Maori War in New Zealand.
1867 End of transportation (shipment of convicts) to Australia.
1870s Dutch control all East Indies (Indonesia).
1872 End of the Maori Wars in New Zealand.
1874 Fiji a British colony.
1879 First Indian workers arrive in Fiji.
1885 Germany and Britain share New Guinea.
1893 Votes for women in New Zealand.
1896 Philippines breaks free from Spanish rule.
1899 USA gains control of Philippines.

MOVEMENTS

Migration

In the 1800s many people from Europe settled in the United States. Smaller numbers went to Canada, Africa, Australia and New Zealand. All these migrants sought a better life, and many also hoped to find freedom from persecution. In the 20th century migrants continued to move from country to country, seeking prosperity. Most immigrants to the USA now come mainly from Latin America and Asia. Migrants from Asia (from Turkey, India, Pakistan and Bangladesh, for example) have also settled in Europe.

Fight for rights and equality

In the 20th century, nations and peoples have suffered and fought for freedom and justice. Women and minority groups have campaigned for equal rights. There have been religious quarrels, racial divisions, and persecution of groups of people by others. One of the world's most urgent problems is the widening gap between the rich and poor nations. Giving people everywhere a fair share of the world's bounty, and at the same time conserving resources for future generations, is probably the greatest challenge facing humanity today.

Search for world peace

In the 1800s people expected wars. Strong nations used war as a means of getting what they wanted. No one believed in the 'glory' of war after the slaughter of the First World War. The League of Nations was founded to resolve disputes between nations peacefully. But Adolf Hitler and other dictators simply ignored the League. After the Second World War, the Allies set up the United Nations. Most nations belong to the UN, but it is not a world government. It has not prevented further wars, but it has helped to end them. UN relief agencies do marvellous work around the world, and the blue flag of a UN peace-keeping force brings hope to people suffering the misery of war.

EUROPE

1905 Revolution in Russia fails.
1912–13 Balkan Wars.
1914–18 World War I.
1917 Russian Revolution.
1920s Chaos in Germany.
1924 Death of Lenin.
1930s Trade slump and unemployment.

Nazi soldier and Swastika 1930s

1933 Hitler becomes leader of Germany.
1936–9 Civil War in Spain.
1939–45 World War II.
1945–8 Communists take over in eastern Europe.
1946 Nuremberg trials of Nazi war criminals.
1948 Berlin airlift (Germany).
1949 Germany divided.
1953 Death of Stalin.
1956 Uprising in Hungary.
1957 Soviets launch first space satellite.
1957 Foundation of European Economic Community (EEC).
1961 East Germans build Berlin Wall.
1961 Yuri Gagarin (USSR), first astronaut.
1968 Soviet Red Army invades Czechoslovakia.
1969 Violence in Northern Ireland.
1973 Britain, Ireland, Denmark join EEC
1981 Greece joins EEC.
1985 New era of reform in USSR.
1986 Spain and Portugal join EEC.
1989 Berlin Wall opened. Collapse of Communism in Eastern Europe.
1990s Germany reunited. Break-up of the USSR. War in former Yugoslavia.

ASIA

1904–5 Japan defeats Russia.
1911 Revolution in China.
1914–18 World War I. Japan joins Allies. Arabs revolt against Turks.
1921 Reza Khan seizes power in Persia.
1922 Last Sultan of Ottoman Turkey deposed.
1923 Turkey a republic under Atatürk.
1927 Civil War in China.
1932 Kingdom of Saudi Arabia founded.
1937 Japan attacks China.
1941 Pearl Harbor; Japan attacks USA.

The Atom Bomb 1944-45

1945 Allies drop atomic bombs on Japan.
1946 Civil war in China.
1946 Start of Vietnamese war against French.
1947 India and Pakistan independent.
1947 Creation of modern Israel.
1949 Indonesia independent.
1949 China becomes Communist.
1950–3 Korean War.
1956 Arab–Israeli War.
1958 Revolution in Iraq,
1966 Cultural Revolution in China.
1967 Six-Day War between Arabs and Israelis.
1972 Ceylon becomes Sri Lanka.
1973 Yom Kippur War (Arab–Israeli).
1974 Partition of Cyprus.
1975 Vietnam War ends. Khmer Rouge seize power in Cambodia.
1975 Civil war in Lebanon.
1979 Islamic revolution in Iran.
1979 Afghanistan invaded by Soviet army.
1979 War between China and Vietnam.
1980s Japan leading world trading nation.
1980–8 Iran–Iraq war.
1989 Chinese government crushes democracy movement.
1990s Gulf War. Middle East peace talks begin between Israelis and Arabs.

AFRICA

1902 Boer War ends in South Africa.
1907 Belgian government takes over Congo colony.
1910 South Africa becomes self-governing Dominion within British Empire.
1911 Italy conquers Libya.
1922 Egypt self-governing.
1935 Italy conquers Ethiopia.
1940s Growth of nationalist movements, demanding independence.

War in the Sahara 1941-43

1941–3 Fighting in North Africa during World War II.
1949 Apartheid in South Africa.
1952 Mau Mau terrorism in Kenya.
1956 Britain and France attack Egypt after Egypt's President Nasser nationalizes Suez Canal.
1957 Ghana (Gold Coast) independent.
1960s Most former colonies in Africa independent. Civil war in Congo.
1961 South Africa becomes a republic.
1965 Rhodesia declares illegal independence.
1967–70 Civil war in Nigeria.
1974 Portuguese colonies (Angola, Mozambique. Guinea-Bissau) become independent.
1979 Fall of Ugandan dictator Idi Amin.
1980 Rhodesia becomes black-ruled Zimbabwe.
1980s Wars and famine ravage North-East and parts of East Africa.
1990s End of apartheid in South Africa. Islamic fundamentalism in North Africa.
1994 Nelson Mandela becomes first black President of South Africa.

AMERICA

1903 Wrights make first flights in powered aircraft.
1910 Civil war in Mexico.
1914 Panama Canal opens.
1917 USA enters World War I.
1919 First transatlantic flight.
1920 Prohibition of alcohol in USA.
1929 Wall Street crash brings financial ruin.
1930s Great Depression; US President Roosevelt's New Deal.
1941 USA enters World War II.
1945 US forces help free Europe from Nazis, drop atomic bombs on Japan to end war.
1952 USA explodes hydrogen bomb.
1956 Cuba's Communist revolution.
1962 Cuban missile crisis.
1963 US President Kennedy assassinated.
1968 US troops in Vietnam War number half a million.
1968 Murders of Martin Luther King and Robert Kennedy (USA).

Man on the Moon 1969

1969 US astronauts land on Moon.
1973 US troops leave Vietnam.
1974 Watergate scandal in USA. President Nixon resigns.
1975 End of Vietnam War.
1980s Wars in El Salvador and Nicaragua.
1982 Falklands War between Britain and Argentina.
1983 US and Caribbean forces invade Grenada.
1989 US invades Panama.
1990s Chile and Brazil return to democratic rule.
1993 William Jefferson Clinton succeeds George Bush as US President.

PACIFIC

1901 Commonwealth of Australia.
1914–18 Australia and New Zealand fight alongside Britain in World War I.
1928 Kingsford Smith (Australia) flies across the Pacific Ocean.
1934 First air service between Britain and Australia.
1939–45 World War II: Australia and New Zealand declare war on Germany, 1939; Japan attacks USA, 1941, conquers much of South-East Asia and Pacific before being defeated.
1951 ANZUS defence treaty signed by Australia, New Zealand and USA.

Across Antarctica 1958

1958 First land crossing of Antarctica.
1960 Antarctic Treaty signed.
1962 Western Samoa independent.
1965 Australian troops fight in Vietnam War.
1967 Suharto succeeds Sukarno as President of Indonesia.
1970 Fiji and Tonga independent,
1972 Ferdinand Marcos imposes army rule in Philippines.
1975 Papua New Guinea independent.
1976 Indonesia takes over Portuguese East Timor.
1979 Kiribati (Gilbert Islands) become independent.
1980 Vanuatu (New Hebrides) become independent.
1980s Australia and New Zealand strengthen economic links with Pacific and Asian neighbours.
1983 Brunei becomes independent.
1986 End of Marcos regime in the Philippines.
1987 Army take-over in Fiji.
1991 Federated States of Micronesia; Marshall Islands independent.

GLOSSARY

alliance Agreement between two or more countries to help one another, often in war.

astronaut US space traveller; in Russian space programme known as a cosmonaut.

bankruptcy Being without money to pay debts.

capitalism Free market economic and social system, based on private ownership.

cavalry Soldiers fighting on horseback.

civil war War between different groups within a country.

Cold War The political hostility between East and West in the 1950s and 1960s.

colony A settlement of people establishing their way of life in another country.

communism Economic and social system based on state ownership.

democracy Government by the people, through elected representatives.

depression Period of economic slump, causing unemployment.

dictator Ruler who is all-powerful and who often governs harshly.

diplomacy Means by which countries deal with one another, by bargaining.

dynasty Ruling family, one generation succeeding another.

empire A large territory ruled by an emperor or king.

fascism Government system which developed in 1920s and 1930s in Italy, Germany and Spain; militaristic, nationalist and intolerant of opposition.

finance Money or tax matters.

frontier Boundary of a country or empire.

fundamentalism Belief in basics or essential truths.

gold rush Arrival of many people hoping to find gold.

guerrillas Fighters in small groups, often from secret hideouts.

Hindu Follower of Hinduism, the main religion of India.

Islam Religion founded by the Prophet Muhammad (died in AD 632).

migrants People moving from country to country, or across a country, in search of a better life.

missionaries People seeking to convert others to their own religious beliefs.

Muslim Follower of **Islam**.

nationalism Movement seeking to advance the power of a particular nation or country.

Ottoman Empire Empire based on Turkey with its capital at Istanbul, until early 1900s.

peasant Poor person working as farm labourer.

Pope The head of the Roman Catholic Christian Church, based in Rome.

radical Person with advanced ideas, a believer in progress.

reform Changes, especially to government or society.

republic Form of government without a king or queen.

refugees People forced from their lands by war, persecution or natural disasters.

revolution The overthrow of one government by people who set up another.

settlers People building homes and farms in a new land.

Shah Title used by Persian and other Muslim rulers.

shogun Military ruler in Japan, until 1860s.

slaves People forced to work for someone; either captives or people born into slavery.

slump see **depression**.

socialism System based on sharing of wealth and property.

stock market Place where shares in businesses are bought and sold.

toleration Allowing others to think and worship as they please.

treaty An agreement between countries or rulers.

Tsar Ruler of Russian Empire until 1917.

United Nations Organization of world states. UN agencies run peacekeeping, education, aid and other operations.

INDEX

Acknowledgements
Designer: Ben White
Project Editor: Lionel Bender
Text Editor: Mike March
Picture Researcher: Jennie Karrach
Media Conversion and Typesetting:
    Peter MacDonald and Una Macnamara.
Managing Editor: David Riley.
All maps by Hayward Art Group.

Picture credits
Title page, Page 3: Lionel Bender. Pages 12, 14: The Bridgemann Art Library. Pages 17, 21, 23: The Hulton-Deutsch Collection. Page 24: Popperfoto. Page 25: The Bridgemann Art Collection. Page 26: The Hulton-Deutsch Collection. Page 27, 29: The Mansell Collection. Page 31: Stephen Penn/The Hutchison Library. Page 33: Popperfoto. Page 34: John Massey Stewart. Page 36: The Hulton-Deutsch Collection. Page 37: Courtesy of the Ford Motor Company Ltd. Page 38-39: Military Archive & Research Services, Lincs. Page 42: TRH Pictures. Page 42: ZEFA. Pages 44: Saturday Evening Post/Retrograph Archive. Page 45: Texaco/Retrograph Archive. Page 49: Popperfoto. Pages 50-51: ZEFA. Page 51: Courtesy of Barclays Bank plc. Pages 52, 53: Martin Jager/Frank Spooner Pictures-Gamma. Page 56: ZEFA. Page 57: Paul Harrison/Panos Pictures.

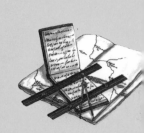

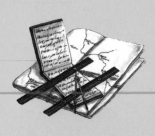